WRITING POETRY

WRITING POETRY

Suggestions for Young Writers

BY

MARIE GILCHRIST

Author of 'Wide Pastures'

WITH POEMS BY MEMBERS OF THE
STEVENSON ROOM POETRY GROUP OF
THE CLEVELAND PUBLIC LIBRARY

Boston and New York
HOUGHTON MIFFLIN COMPANY
The Riverside Press Cambridge
1932

The Riverside Press
CAMBRIDGE · MASSACHUSETTS
PRINTED IN THE U.S.A.

TO
THE STEVENSON ROOM POETRY GROUP
AND ITS GODPARENTS
IN THE
CLEVELAND PUBLIC LIBRARY

LINDA ANNE EASTMAN
MARILLA WAITE FREEMAN
ANNIE SPENCER CUTTER
JEAN CAROLYN ROOS
BESSIE HOLMES KELSEY

Good poetry seems so simple and natural a thing that when we meet it we wonder that all men are not always poets.   Poetry is nothing but healthy speech.

HENRY DAVID THOREAU

PREFACE

A few years ago it fell to me, as an assistant in the Stevenson Room for Young People in the Cleveland Public Library, to direct a group of high-school boys and girls who had asked for 'a poetry club.' When I asked them what they wanted to do, they said almost unanimously that they wanted to write poetry, and I was nonplussed. I had no large confidence in their abilities, and less in my capacity to help them. I considered the discipline of poetry a private and solitary pursuit. But I had a firm belief in the value of poetry, and this was enough for a start. Fat notebooks filled with their own productions indicated how much poetry meant to some of these youngsters. It was a robust interest which survived the competition of school and social activities, bringing them downtown — an hour's ride on the trolley for a few of them — every other Friday night during the school year.

Feeling my way blindly and asking the group pretty often what they wanted, I went ahead. The group dwindled in size. Somewhat bewildered but persistent, the remnant and I clung to each other for the rest of the term. We were reënforced by new recruits the following fall, and the loose-leaf

notebook in which their better efforts were pre-
served lost its lank look. Now a second volume is
well under way, for, with a fluctuating attendance,
the Stevenson Room Poetry Group has survived
for four years and is still active. It has never had
any organization or definite membership. New
members enter at any time, others drop out, while
some remain until college takes them from us. One
small anthology, 'Preludes to Poetry,' has been
printed, and to our astonishment an edition of five
hundred copies was rapidly sold out.

Obviously, I did not teach these young people to
write poetry. 'How do you get poetry out of them?'
I have been asked. When I repeated that remark
to the group, they were much amused. They knew
that poetry was not to be extracted. Once, when I
was wanting a title for an article on the group, I
happened to re-read Robert Frost's 'Pasture
Spring':

> I'm going out to clean the pasture spring;
> I'll only stop to rake the leaves away
> (And wait to watch the water clear, I may):
> I shan't be gone long. You come too.

Then I took 'Uncovering Springs' for my title.
It came nearest to expressing what I hoped to do
for these boys and girls who came to the group
meetings because they loved poetry and wanted to

write it. If they had not cared for it, I would have tried first to communicate to them some of my own enthusiasm for poetry. I could have begun by teaching them to scan lines, have given them a variety of verse patterns, put a rhyming dictionary in their hands, and trained them to write technically correct verse. But that would not have started them on the road to writing genuine poetry.

As it was, I used every resource at my command to widen and clear their conception of poetry. Some of them had a jingle and rhyme notion of it, derived perhaps from their earliest reading lessons. My resources were a long practice in writing poetry, considerable study, and an indestructible love of it. To this I added all that I could find out about the way other writers went at their work, and what psychologists had to say of artists and the creative impulse.

I talked to the group about originality, showing them how that quality is inevitably present in every individual. I proved to them how the best writers drew their imagery and their ideas from their own experience and associations, and that the poor poets used stock phrases, stock ideas.

A simple amateur word-association test revealed to them what different things the same word could suggest to different people. I passed around their old manuscripts one evening and asked them to mark the worn phrases. These were brought to judgment, read aloud and approved or condemned by the group, and such bad pennies as 'smiles and tears,' 'hopes and fears,' and at least twenty others were outlawed.

With short pieces of poetic prose and prose translations of foreign poetry (Greek, Latin, Japanese, and American Indian furnished some of the best examples), I showed them how poetry lay not in rhyme and meter, but in the fusion of two unlike things — generally a piece of human experience and a glimpse of life or nature perceived by the senses — a representation of one thing in terms of another.

Mary Austin's 'American Rhythm' helped to show them how poetry varied according to a people's occupation, environment, and ways of thinking. I used folk poetry as much as possible in my illustrations, since that was the least artificial and yet rich in varied forms, and showed the fine results which follow when a genuine feeling is expressed in terms of a bred-in-the-bone environment. I emphasized that the most time-honored forms began as units of words and rhythms shaped to some unit of feeling and thought, and that, while these forms would serve again in many cases, new ones could yet be conceived which might better suit a new time and other people.

When, as sometimes happened, a new member wanted to 'take up' sonnets and have the group write sonnets in unison, I replied that if he was sufficiently interested, he would practice such forms independently, and that I should be glad to discuss the completed exercise; but that to approach poetry by fixed forms of verse was to act as if the shell were created before the egg. Not that a knowledge of the established forms of verse is unimportant; but a little knowledge acquired through a conscious need of it is worth more than an attic full of unemployed information. The healthy mind goes in search of the nourishment it craves, and no true craftsman will long lack tools he feels the need of to carry out his idea.

So much for the theory and technique of poetry. All the time, but rarely at every meeting, the different members brought in verses that they had written. I read these aloud to the group and called for discussion. If there was none forthcoming, I began the criticism with a comment or a question. Did the writer say what he intended to say? Was the idea clear and complete? Did the words fit? Was the poem too long? Long poems, rambling on until the death of the hero or the mention of eternity brought them to a conclusion, became less prevalent. So did mere descriptions. Short poems concentrated in single images began to appear.

I told members of the group not to write until they had the germ of an idea to develop, and I made them notice the endings of poems particularly — how the best poems always closed with special point and emphasis because they were complete conceptions in the writers' minds. I gave them no long list of technical weaknesses to avoid, but instead, urged them to put into their own words all the vigor and warmth that an experience held for them. They soon realized that the writing done when they strained and wrestled with a faint inspiration or a feeble idea was the victim of parasitic imagery, jerky rhythms, and unnatural, constricted arrangements of words.

For a time we explored the poetry of other countries in translation. We were able, through the abilities of the group, to hear French, German, Greek, Latin, and Hebrew poetry read in the original. Older visitors were rarely allowed unless they had something to contribute. In this way we once heard Dutch poetry read and translated, and French, German, and Negro songs sung to music. I generally brought to the meetings whatever new poetry I had discovered; the group members brought in poems that they liked. Sometimes they asked me to read and discuss special poets or certain types of verse. One year I had a definitely planned series of topics for each meeting; another year I al-

lowed chance to direct us, and chance always furnished something pertinent.

It is very easy to lapse into law-giving when
younger people ask to be instructed. I tried to
counter this by the frequent refrain: 'This is only
my opinion and cannot be final. What Keats says,
what Robert Frost and Amy Lowell and Ezra
Pound, what Walt Whitman and Wordsworth say,
can only show us how *they* approached the problem
of poetry.'

By means of these meetings the members were
exposed to a vast amount of good poetry. The free
discussion of the group (and this flourishes best
when there are as many boys as girls) helped to
disembarrass them, so that they found it easier
than they had imagined to hear their writings read
and dissected. I was in the same boat — they
knew that I also tried to write; and so we felt easy
with one another, we learned to take laughter at
our own expense. Furthermore, they realized the
happiness which is to be found in free and honest
expression whatever the medium. They gained
that advance in technique which only eager, self-
imposed practice can give.

The following chapters are in line with my talks
to the Stevenson Room Poetry Group. The poems
will introduce to you some of the members of the
group. Credit for these poems belongs to the writ-

ers, but immediate stimulus for many of them was received from school classes and clubs. A number of them have been printed in Cleveland school and college periodicals.

CLEVELAND, OHIO
  March, 1932

CONTENTS

WRITING POETRY

WRITING POETRY

I

LANGUAGE

Words are hoops
Through which to leap upon meanings
Which are horses' backs,
Bare, moving.

WITTER BYNNER

COMMUNICATION is possibly the basic reason for art. Great artists communicate widely and completely while lesser artists mumble to themselves. Poetry is concerned with the communication of feeling, with the telling of experiences for which there is no single word. It does something more than telling. It thrusts a piece of human experience into your hands with the admonition: 'Here, feel this! Taste it, smell it, think it!'

E. A. Robinson has said: 'Poetry is a language which tells us through a more or less emotional reaction something that cannot be said.'

If poetry is a language, how does it differ from the language we use daily? It is the same language used in a special way. The poet does not speak to us face to face, but we feel as if he were doing so, though he speaks from a great distance and often even from other centuries. This is because he has, in a way, electrified his words with feeling and imagination. They have an immediate tingling effect upon us like contact with a live wire, and they are so evenly interfused that they seem to flow and shine like the copper wire along which an electrified message travels. Every true poem is like a private wire annihilating distance and time.

A single word in a line, a happy epithet, will not accomplish this. We know those futile word-hunters who bring home one large dead epithet in a bag. The power and emphasis of our message depends upon the close relationship that we have formed for our words, upon their perfect fusion.

Every word, of course, has its own meaning, its own possibilities in relationship with other words, its individuality. Some words have been used so constantly in one connection that they stand for more than their actual meaning and it is well to count that extra meaning in, when you use them. G. H. Rylands has pointed out that the moon stands for fate and the mutability of life; that bright is the poetic word for young, beautiful, alive; that the rose is the symbol of loveliness; and precious stones, gold and silver, for that which is greatly desired; summer for perfection; green for romance. Many other words are heavily freighted: dark, for instance, which is perhaps Walter de la Mare's favorite word; spring, meaning youth and love; winter, meaning bareness, death, and dearth; autumn and harvest for ripeness, fulfillment; coin, for every type of exchange and barter. Your meaning can benefit or suffer from these echoing words according to the way you use them.

Other words have become tarnished through usage: *silly*, for example, which used to mean simple, innocent. The German word *selig* — blessed — came from the same root. Some words have taken on dignity with the years. And it is only when you know the ancestry and the history of a word that you can make the best use of it. With its whole meaning active, it will glow like fire-new copper.

Herbert Spencer, the scientist, complained that early speech had a serious defect — 'the lack of words free from implications of vitality.' This may be sad for the scientist, but it is all to the poet's advantage. It is exactly why the old short words of Anglo-Saxon derivation are especially full of meaning. Words that suggest life, movement, form, taste, color, touch, when they are accurately and appropriately used, give life and color and shape to the inner world of thought and feeling.

He left the past year's dwelling for the new,
Stole with soft step its shining archway through,
      Built up its idle door,
Stretched in his last-found home, and knew the old no
    more.
        (O. W. Holmes, 'The Chambered Nautilus.')

Yet old and simple words are not always to be preferred above all others. 'Absolutely the only test of the poetic quality of a word is its ability to hold its own triumphantly in its particular poetic setting,' J. L. Lowes has said. In music some people can instantly recognize a false note because it is 'off key.' In writing, it is the same. Certain types of diction are like notes in a certain scale. These words follow one another as naturally as the notes in a song, and, when a word is inserted that has no natural connections or associations with the rest, it is discordant, and the thread of melody is broken. Exactly upon this sudden note in another key do some writers depend for their effect, humorous or dramatic. Dorothy Parker does this when she changes to slang or profanity.

Three be the things I shall have till I die,
Laughter and hope and a sock in the eye.
        ('Inventory.')

A feeling for language can be developed by observing whenever you read whether the words used

seem too showy or too shabby for the occasion:
whether they help or hinder the flow of meaning,
and if their course is consistent with the manner of
thinking. Angry thinking, for instance, goes in
jerks or tumbles like a steep brook, and the words
conveying it would naturally move in the same
fashion. Joy of its very nature has a singing quality. Mr. Rylands gives as a test for the use of the
commonplaces of poetic diction and roundabout
expressions: 'All depends upon the motive, upon
whether they are employed to delight or as a dis-
guise, from a sense of beauty or a sense of shame.'
The conviction that much of our language was too
vulgar for poetry caused many dismal evasions
during the last century, while Shakespeare gives us
our greatest examples of the most vulgar words so
perfectly used that they become noble poetry.

There can be no rule for what words to use and
what to avoid. Wordsworth decided that he
wanted to use only the words of common speech,
but his best poetry is not limited to such diction.
Then he used the words that best carried his meaning. The writer, not knowing his audience, can in
fairness only assume that it is neither more nor less
intelligent than himself. He will use words which
the greatest number of people will understand —
neither technical, high-sounding nor bookish, without cant or slang — unless he is dramatizing char-

acters who would naturally use such language; though even then the artist uses it sparingly.

Words whose meanings have been almost worn out will be about as useless as dead bulbs in the spelling of an electric sign. At first they may seem exactly the words to use for poetry because they have appeared there so often before. But the life of poetry lies in fresh relationships between words, in the spontaneous fusion of hitherto unrelated words. Such things must take place in your own head, by your own chemistry.

Some words have already been put together so often that they occur joined in our thought: *days of yore*, for instance; *empty dream*, *leafy trees*, *lilting tune*, *sobbing waves*, *hopes and fears*, and so on. It is impossible to reduce these terms to a fluid state, they cannot be made over completely into the fresh substance of your thought; and people call them *clichés*, rubber-stamp words.

There are certain ways of speech so alien to everyday usage or inappropriate to the spirit of our times that we do not expect to find them in good writing: abbreviations such as *ne'er* for *never*, *e'en* for *even*, *'till*, *'tis*, and the old bookish adverbs and connectives — *ere*, *thereunto*, *whither*, *thither*, and so forth. In our speech they sound clumsy except where we are re-creating the atmosphere of a time when those expressions were natural. The old second-person-singulars, *thee* and *thou*, and their accompanying verb-forms, *hast* and *wast*, *doest* and *doth*, belong to the past and to the Quakers. They once seemed especially fitted to high thoughts and elevated emotional expressions, perhaps because they are Biblical. Now we depend upon the simplicity of our diction and the accuracy of our imagery to carry the exact tone of our feelings. We do not capitalize and address the abstractions, Hope, Faith, Love, Friendship, Death, and so on. This is no hard-and-fast rule, but you are competing with the dead rather than the living when you write in this style. Of course any so-called rule in writing may be broken if you are sure enough of your meaning and your purpose to take the risk, provided you remain intelligible.

Your words go into the mind of your reader according to the order in which you have arranged them. If that order is so unexpected as to make re-reading necessary, you have wasted just so much of his energy and interest; you have kinked the wire of your thought. Every language has its own natural order for words and this order changes and grows with the people who use it. As soon as there began to be a United States of America, an American language had its beginning. English literature for a long time dominated conscious American writing, but the rigors and limitations of pioneer living worked their way directly into human speech, and an American language was born. Nowadays, because many of us were born to another language or heard broken English or a foreign language spoken in childhood, words are being put together according to the ways of other languages. In so far as this is a natural expression of the individual, it is good. It keeps our speech vigorous and limber when it does not go against the grain of the language, for beauty and meaning suffer when the individuality of a language is violated.

Your thought and the words that carry it should always advance. If you invert your words, the reason should lie in the emphasis gained or a sudden turn of thought and feeling — never the lazy mechanical convenience of keeping the metre regular or making a rhyme. Language, like music, has the advantage of painting and sculpture where movement is concerned. Reading and writing have inevitably a forward movement; we can unfold action in words. Edna St. Vincent Millay's final sonnet in 'Fatal Interview,' in fact, nearly synchronizes words and action:

Oh, sleep forever in the Latmian cave,
Mortal Endymion, darling of the Moon!

Her silver garments by the senseless wave
Shouldered and dropped and on the shingle strewn,
Her fluttering hand against her forehead pressed,
Her scattered looks that trouble all the sky,
Her rapid footsteps running down the west —
Of all her altered state, oblivious lie!

Words can also give thought actually growing; they can show emotion welling and subsiding, changing its nature, terminating in knowledge and understanding. Movement, then, and representations of the human consciousness undergoing experience are the especial province of writing as an art. More intellectual than music, it can attain a clear, swift flowing of thought and feeling.

Consequently, verbs and words derived from verbs are of great importance. When you say that your object does something, rather than that it is something or like something else, you give it life and movement. Nouns stand for ideas, names, and things. Each noun is a complete picture. Nouns and verbs are almost pure metal. Adjectives are cheaper ore; they have less strength of meaning, since they stand for just one aspect of a thing, one characteristic, and do not represent it in its entirety. They describe rather than re-create, defining for us the proportions of things, color, texture, quality, sorts of action. Many of them, made out of nouns, have the value of similes; those made out of participles, the liveliness of verbs. Much of their value depends, I think, upon the way they space out our thought, which, moving across nouns and verbs alone, goes swiftly. Adjectives slacken its pace just as the small details of a flower or a bird along the road delay one's progress. They can enrich your thought or thin it, according to the way they are used. They can add to the total effect by their accuracy and clear beauty, by their quality of lingering; or they can mar it by their lumpish presences, contributing nothing but additional syllables to the line.

It is a temptation to fill a line with adjectives. They do not affect the grammatical structure; they are easily added and subtracted. They allow you to gloat (and someone has said that poetry is a kind of gloating) over your subject. So Emily Dickinson observed the first arbutus:

> Pink, small, punctual,
> Aromatic, low,
> Covert in April,
> Candid in May....

But often the chaotic enthusiasm which spends itself in adjectives is better compressed into a single sharp image before the poem is begun. It is only on the way, in the adjective stage.

Too many adjectives give the confusion and hard definiteness of a photograph, leaving nothing to the reader's imagination. The poet strives for a stripped accuracy of statement which will leave areas of clean space where the reader's imagination may find exercise.

> To make a prairie it takes a clover and one bee —
> And revery.
> The revery alone will do
> If bees are few.
>
> (EMILY DICKINSON.)[1]

Connectives and articles are unimportant words and should always be inconspicuous unless the meaning calls for emphasis upon them; they should be seen and not heard. Prepositions should be used with great exactness. They are the relationship words and have subtle powers of distinction. Notice how *into* in these lines, adds depth and density to the snow:

> Then might I sniff the stormy wind
> Never for pastures left behind
> But as a fawn goes, might I go
> Like a blown leaf into the falling snow.
>
> (FRANCES FROST, 'Creature.')

Your choice and arrangement of words should always be prompted by a deeper motive than that

[1] Quoted with the permission of Little, Brown and Company.

of intellectual selection. 'A complete poem is one where an emotion has found its thought and the thought has found the words,' Robert Frost has said. Our expressions are as sure and as adequate as our experience. If we are powerfully affected by something we want to communicate, we naturally use live terms because the thing was active in our consciousness. In a moment of keen mental activity we do not use unnecessary words, we do not say things in the passive voice without wanting a distinct impression of passivity, we do not use fumbling imagery.

To quote Robert Henri: 'It is not enough to have thought great things *before* doing the work. The brush stroke at the moment of contact carries inevitably the exact state of being of the artist at the exact moment into the work, and there it is to be seen and read by those who can read such signs, and to be read later by the artist himself with perhaps some surprise, as a revelation of himself.'

Whether we write in lyrical fashion and say *I* and *You*, or whether, like Shakespeare, we put a wealth of observation and experience into characters we have invented, we are yet making a personal revelation. In a sense, every sort of writer proclaims continually: 'This is how it strikes me.' Even in ordinary conversation we unconsciously

select those things which seem to us the most significant or delightful. This individual selecting
process is art. We tell an incident best when we
are entirely engrossed in representing it clearly and
truthfully and are not airing a grudge on the side
or defending ourselves. This is 'emotion recollected in tranquillity' — Wordsworth's definition
of poetry. But have you known any conversation
more delightful and moving than that of the person
who can see the funny and tragic, the lovable and
despicable in one human being and tell you about
him briefly and vividly? That is the art of the
greatest novelists and poets. It has its roots in a
nature both honest and generous. The nearer we
come to the actual in proportioning and interrelat-
ing all sorts of human motives, the greater artists
we shall be.

Robert Frost once classified literature in the
following manner:

Uncommon in experience — uncommon in writing.

Common in experience — common in writing.
Uncommon in experience — common in writing.
Common in experience — uncommon in writing.

This last, he said, made the best writing. The
uncommonness in writing showed that the writer's
essential originality had been at work, tempering

his metal in his own furnaces, beating his words into fine wires vibrant with meaning.

Have you heard telephone wires along a country road humming in the wind some cold morning? That is how your lines should sing.

II

IMAGERY

The one indispensable talent for creative art, whether of the theater or literature or music or plastic representation, is the talent for experiencing.

MARY AUSTIN

A TALENT for experiencing is sometimes confused with an appetite for thrills, which is really its opposite. The thrill-hunter avoids the full impact of any experience. The truth of the matter is that any sort of life, however uneventful, is a deep and unescapable experience. Much of its humdrum quality is due only to our being afraid to participate in situations directly confronting us.

When we speak of experience, we think of exceptional happenings, though for writing, every moment we have lived counts, and serves us in one way or another. We cannot define experience as certain emotional crises. Love, marriage, birth, death, the failure of years of effort, are naturally the big turning-points of life, but surely most of us can remember situations in our childhood when emotions such as these crises call forth have been aroused. Unfortunately, children are rarely permitted the dignity of their emotions; they are hushed and petted out of them instead of given a chance to live their way through them. Experience is defined in Webster's Collegiate Dictionary as 'the actual living through an event or events.' And it is just this sense of coming through something, this growth in consciousness, that gives rise to poetry.

Much of the writing of young people is condemned by the wholesale statement, 'They have nothing to say,' and then condoned by 'They haven't had enough experience.' They may not have the emotional reactions of a mature person, but they have much to say. A child less than four years old had new things to say about music:

> Some music is bended and patting,
> And sorry for spanked children;
> And some is awful,
> Made with elbows and not fingers.
> It tells dogs to bite,
> And children to tear up books....

(NANNCE. *The New Republic*, June 17, 1931.)

If, instead of experience, we said that young writers lacked confidence in the integrity of their own emotions, their own point of view, we should come nearer the truth. They read poetry and think that their feelings should echo those already expressed by older writers. If they could only realize that fresh feeling and thinking and a new emotional approach to life are what the world craves!

Poetry has been defined in a great number of ways, but one characteristic, found where the word is used in its broadest sense as an aspect of any way of life, lies in the vitality and freshness of that aspect — a new way of looking at things. All of us are entitled to this, simply by that unique combination of personality and circumstance which makes up each individual's existence, but many people draw no fresh conclusions, perhaps because they find it more convenient not to differ from their fellows, or because they fear the untried and satisfy themselves with custom and hearsay. When we passively receive other people's ideas and conform to them, we are not really living. Our experience is hardly our own; it bears no fruit in thought and conduct. But when feeling reacts freely and naturally upon thought, something new is created. The receptive mind, stirred by an impression, forms a separate and original idea, revealing the thinker's personality and the quality of the impression as surely as the nature of a child reflects its forebears.

Do you remember how, as a child, you amused the grown-ups or startled them with the observations you made upon their conduct? Eventually you learned to keep these more to yourself, since laughter or sometimes scoldings and punishments followed, pruning and training the green budding shoots of an original point of view into the preferred pattern.

Children describe and identify everything new by the terms and images already familiar to them. They have fewer things in their minds with which to compare a new object or sensation and so they associate dissimilar things by a wider stretch of the imagination than that made by the more practical adult mind. This is exactly what good poetry does. The artistic imagination has been said to see likenesses; the scientific, differences. The greatest poets, I think, see both, and so are able to represent life with the utmost fidelity.

From the time when the light first shines in our unfocused baby eyes we are continually storing up impressions, and these are our greatest resource, for art. Willa Cather, whose novels are luminous with the poetry of experience, once said: 'I think that most of the basic material a writer works with is acquired before the age of fifteen.'

Our recollection of some poignant experience is closely bound up with the external details of that day, that moment, when those memorable words were said, when that thing happened, which changed life somehow. That feeling and the sunlight slanting through the doorway, or the scent of a certain flower, or the feel of rain in the air, the pattern of a wall-paper — sensuous images all of them — are associated for us, and keep the power of recalling each other until later associations blur or blot out their relationship.

So, if you are representing a certain mood or experience, whether you call it your own or that of a character you have invented, images will come to your mind to express that feeling which are unlike anyone else's. Other people will have the same feeling aroused in them when they read your words because the connection is a true one.

Besides these natural deposits of impressions deep in your consciousness to draw upon for poetry, something else is active, directing your choice of imagery. Unconsciously, your mood at the time of creation focuses your attention upon objects which are harmonious to it. So the murderer, seeing a spot of red in the distance, will think of blood, while the child imagines that he sees his toy engine, a flower, or his mother's dress. On days when we are at odds with ourselves and the world, the very houses along the street appear dingy, the faces of the passers-by ugly and sad; and another time, when our feet fairly dance along the pavement toward some delightful prospect, what fascinating things we observe in the shop windows, what happy faces along the way! Beauty and ugliness were both present each day, but something inside us focused the lenses of our attention very differently. It is no small task to keep these lenses clear, accurately focused. It needs delicate adjustments steadily maintained, it requires health of mind and body. And, after these are secured, to record an experience as it reached you in all its color, its native imagery, you must have the power of sustained concentration.

One of the members of the Poetry Group was describing the shadows cast by trees on moonlit water. She wrote first:

> ... tree-etchings
> Shivering on drowsy water.

And then she lost confidence in her choice of the word *shivering*. She had not seen it used of shadows before and she thought it might sound queer. So she struggled until she achieved the stereotyped line,

> Shimmering on moonlit water.

It was work wasted. She did not have to work to find 'Shivering on drowsy water,' except for the task of concentrating on the picture her mind had once received, because the tree shadows had actually 'shivered' to her mind when she saw them.

Early in this century a certain group of poets took the name of Imagists and published a creed. It wasn't very revolutionary, but it is worth considering.

'1. To use the language of common speech, but to employ always the *exact* word, not the merely decorative word.

'2. To create new rhythms — as the expression of new moods. We do not insist upon "free verse" as the only method of writing poetry — we do believe that the individuality of a poet may often be better expressed in free verse than in conventional forms.

'3. To allow absolute freedom in the choice of subject.

'4. To present an image (hence the name Imagist). We are not a school of painters, but we believe that poetry should render particulars exactly and not deal in vague generalities, however magnificent and sonorous.

'5. To produce poetry that is hard and clear, never blurred or indefinite.

'6. Finally, most of us believe that concentration is the very essence of poetry.'

This concentration is the crystallizing process by which the poet secures clear, original images. It takes him past the levels of conscious memory, where he recalls the things other poets have said of a similar subject, into the layered coal and fossil and quartz deposits of his own impressions.

The person who has the greatest wealth of images is, usually, the person with the most acute senses. Nowadays, when there is so much noise going on about us to which we instinctively close our thought, our images are derived more from our eyes' experience than our ears'. Perhaps we are self-conscious and find it easier to observe un-noticed than to hear and taste and touch. It is the Little Pitchers and Meddlesome Matties and Greedy Gutses of a generation ago who are now recording sense impressions vividly.

Shakespeare is one of the few poets as alive to sound and touch as to sight. Much of his power lies in the fact that he appeals to several senses at once:

> ... Three winters cold
> Have from the forest shook three summers' pride,
> Three beauteous springs to yellow autumn turn'd
> In process of the seasons have I seen.
> Three April perfumes in three hot Junes burn'd,
> Since first I saw you fresh which yet are green....
>
> (Sonnet 104.)

Part of Keats's rich sensuousness comes from his keen perceptions of touch and taste images:

> To bend with apples the mossed cottage trees,
> And fill all fruit with ripeness to the core;
> To swell the gourd, and plump the hazel shells
> With a sweet kernel....
>
>   ('Ode to Autumn.')

What a feeling he has for the textures of things, for surfaces, for the silken quality of flowers and leaves and grasses, for fabrics and flesh!

Rudyard Kipling uses the sharp recalling power of odors in 'Lichtenberg':

> And I saw Sydney the same as ever,
>   The picnics and brass-bands;
> And my little homestead on Hunter River
>   And my new vines joining hands.
> It all came over me in one act
>   Quick as a shot through the brain —
> With the smell of the wattle round Lichtenberg
>   Riding in, in the rain.

Robert Browning's live warmth is often due to his use of the characteristic motions of human beings for symbols:

> Oh, good gigantic smile o' the brown old earth
> This autumn morning!
>
>   ('Among the Rocks.')

Images that represent muscular reactions are particularly powerful. They can be so brief, and yet we almost feel them along our own nerves.

Using as a figure, her small sister asleep beside her, one member of the Poetry Group made a vivid representation of memory:

> At night
> The warm body of memory
> Lies close to me.
> Too close....
> So fretfully
> I push it away.
>
> (DOROTHY AMDUR.)

A very poignant way of representing an emotion is to give the muscular tensions used to suppress or control feeling. It is one of the actor's most telling devices. And it is found in this Japanese *hokku*, seventeen syllables long:

> At parting
> I spoke
> By pressing hard with my fingertips
> On what was nearest me.
>
> (AKIKO YOSANO.)

The shorter, the more compact an image is, the greater its intensity. We get it in a flash. So a metaphor that takes an active characteristic of one thing and transfers it to another is stronger than a simile. But the slower motion of the simile is sometimes desirable. It is more meditative than a metaphor.

The Assyrian came down like a wolf on the fold

has the lope of a four-footed animal in its rhythm, and the image of the wolf, in a sense, lopes into our minds. But if we said

> The Assyrian wolfed down upon them —

this impression would be spoiled, though the concentration of *wolfed* adds fierceness to the image.

People have used similes since the beginnings of speech. Before there were many words, prehistoric men must have pointed to one object and then another and eyed each other and grunted, indicating a discovery of likeness. The Bible and the long romances of the Middle Ages are full of stock similes: *black as coal, white as snow, swift as a bird*. Our very language is rich in words that are fossil similes. If you have read any translation of Homer's Iliad, you will remember how often he used *wine-dark* to describe the sea. *Ruby-red, snowy, bird-like, steely*, are a few that come immediately to mind. They make a comparison without including the machinery of the phrase *like a* and project your idea more swiftly and smoothly.

The value of the simile lies in the originality with which it is used, the happy chance of its association. Chaucer used many of the old stock similes, but somehow gave them a touch of freshness by the way he worded them. Other similes are so obviously the product of his own delighted

eyes that we know just how those objects looked,
to Chaucer:

> She was full morë blissful on to seë
> Than is the newë pear-jonettë treë
> And softer than the wool is of a wether.

You will catch Chaucer's rhythm if you pronounce
the final *e*, where it is marked, as an extra syllable.
The widow's cock Chauntecleer had a *very* merry
voice, to Chaucer's mind:

> His voice was merrier than the merry organ...
>
> His comb was redder than the fine corál...
>
> His nails were whiter than the lily flower.

You can add dignity or ludicrousness to your
thought by a simile or a metaphor. They must
first of all be, to a certain extent, reasonable. They
must not suggest impossibilities at which our imaginations balk. And they must never be mixed. If
the image we use is not clear in our minds, we are
very likely to mix two figures, which is as bad as
making two exposures on one film.

The actual size or magnitude of the objects
which you use in comparison has a great deal to do
with the effect of your simile or metaphor. The
grandeur and power of Robinson Jeffers's poetry is
partly derived from the large proportions of the
objects he uses for his images. Its spaciousness

depends upon the grand, slow, elemental processes
of nature which he constantly pictures:

The world has many seas, Mediterranean, Atlantic, but
    here is the shore of the one ocean.
And here the heavy future hangs like a cloud; the enor-
    mous scene; the enormous games preparing
Weigh on the water and strain the rock; the stage is
    here, the play is conceived, the players are not
    found.

('Contrast.')

You lessen the effect of outdoor things, for instance, if you describe them in terms of the in-
doors; if you carpet and curtain your forest —
unless, of course, you want the effect of a room emphasized. Sufficient contrast is needed between
the objects compared to make the similarity strik-
ing, but never incongruous. For objects have their
kingdoms, Animal, Vegetable, and Mineral, like
the old game; and a shadow of that realm will
follow each image, proportioning the total effect.

Havelock Ellis wrote: 'It was a fine and deep
saying of Aristotle's that "the greatest thing by
far is to be a master of metaphor." This is the
mark of genius, for, said he, it implies an intuitive
perception of the similarity in dissimilars. All the
great thinkers have been masters of metaphor, because all vivid thinking must be in images, and the

philosopher whose metaphors are blurred or diluted is the one whose thinking is blurred or diluted. Thus it comes about that the thinkers who survive are the thinkers who wrote well and are most nearly poets. Not that they need have attained to that which we, individually or collectively, may be pleased to consider "Truth." But they were alive; they had realized what they meant; they embodied their thoughts in definite images which are a perpetual challenge to thought for all who come after.'

'They had realized what they meant' — that is the prime essential for poetry, for clear imagery. That is what kindled the fire in the parables of Christ, the prose of Tolstoy and Thoreau, and all enduring poetry.

III

RHYTHM

Of rhythm in general the most significant thing that we can say is this, that it seems to be always present where there is life.

SIR HENRY NEWBOLT

RHYTHM of some sort is essential to all continuance of life (continuance in fact implies rhythm), beginning with the regular beat of our hearts, the cadence of our breathing. A failing rhythm counsels us that disintegration and death are at hand; an irregular rhythm indicates struggle and conflict; a mechanically regular beat, the absence of normal emotion; and a harmonious rhythm, somewhat regular but individual, is the basic pattern and symbol of all that is lovely in life. It is the first essential for any art.

Rhythm is the truest indicator of what is actually being felt or experienced. A physician first consults his patient's rhythms of blood and breath to find out what is wrong with him. The veracity of the statements of men on trial has been calculated by machines which register the altered throbbing of their pulses under the excitement of various questions. A poet's words tell us something about him, but his rhythms tell us far more. We cannot help responding to them even though we are intellectually blind to their meaning. Sometimes poets confuse us by employing rhythms which contradict their words. Then we know that the poetry is faked.

'Moving rhythm in poetry,' says Mr. I. A. Richards, 'rises only from genuinely stirred impulses.'

No two persons' rhythms are absolutely alike, because no two lives can be entirely similar. Just as one man's steps are longer or shorter than another's and as he moves and speaks more swiftly or slowly; as he is more or less in harmony with himself and his environment; according to the way he reacts emotionally — just so will his words emerge in rhythms peculiar to him. Painters speak of line, space, and color rhythms in a landscape. Poets also feel these harmonies and adopt them unconsciously. Some people would say that Wordsworth found his inspiration in the grandeur and beautiful variety of the Lake Country; others, that the rhythms of that country passed into his poetry. Songs made by the American Indians who lived among the hills and woods have a greater variety of rhythms than those made by the Indians of the desert with its monotony of line and color. Our manual occupations fall into definite beats and swings, and these, too, repeat themselves in poetry. In her book, 'The American Rhythm,'

Mrs. Mary Austin tells how the new life and con-
tours of this country made different rhythms for
its settlers:

'Life set itself to new processions of seed-time
and harvest, the skin newly tuned to seasonal variations, the very blood humming to new altitudes.
The rhythm of walking, always a recognizable
background for our thoughts, altered from the
militaristic stride to the jog of the wide unrutted
earth. Explorer, fur-trader, king's agent, whoever
for three centuries followed it, must have carried a
record of its foot-work in his walk, a wider swing
and recovery to his mind. As the pioneer track
made westward-flowing patterns, the rhythm of
horseback riding, of a rise and fall distinctively of
the American continent, superseded the footpace.
Now and then one picks it up in the work of Vachel
Lindsay and Carl Sandburg, and not only the sad-
dle jog, but the unintermittent cluck and roll of
the Overland Flyer.'

These rhythms of environment and daily living
also affect the cadences which are of profound importance in poetry — the rhythms of emotional
speech. Take a few short utterances at random
and see how differently they are patterned:

> I tell you I won't stand it any longer!
>
> Isn't it lovely to be out of doors?
>
> If you only knew how much I love you.

Notice, too, how the emotion and the idea throw the accent upon certain words which, in another arrangement and with another feeling back of them, would be unemphasized.

Many English words have a definite accent and these give vigor and character to our poetry, and make versifying more difficult, for the accents must not be wrenched when we go about fitting them into a regular pattern. American speech, moreover, has its own accents, more inherent in phrases than in single words. These go deeper than the quaint pronunciations of dialect in representing the spirit of their own place and people. They are truly homespun. Writers are just beginning to recognize and establish in unmistakable rhythms the accents, the individual turns characteristic of the speech of New England, the Western Plains, the South, the mountains of Kentucky and Virginia, the Middle West. Here again the point of relationship comes in. The beauty of these various accents consists in their close relationship to their environments and the people that speak them. They belong exclusively to the matter which they express, and their beauty lies in that belonging.

The emotions have their rhythms, but they are not regular. When we are deeply affected, we are disturbed. It is — to borrow a figure from Mr.

I. A. Richards — as if the various pendulums and polarized needles that determine the balance of our personalities had received some sharp impetus from without that sets them swinging in wider, strongly agitated circles. As the experience ceases reverberating, we settle back into rhythm — a rhythm somewhat changed by the incorporation of this new experience, but regular. This is that ordering of experience which Mr. Richards thinks so characteristic of the poet. The natural representation of ourselves under emotional pressure, then, would be those irregular agitated rhythms swinging back toward regularity.

The poetry which is 'emotion recollected in tranquillity' has the regularity of regained rhythm. The more ecstatic poetry represents a keen emotional moment; a small circle of rhythms lifted by the nature of ecstasy quite out of the ordinary rhythms. So the even spirals of Shelley's verses ascend like the skylark he is celebrating:

> Hail to thee, blithe Spirit!
>   Bird thou never wert,
> That from heaven, or near it,
>   Pourest thy full heart
> In profuse strains of unpremeditated art.
>
> Higher still and higher
>   From the earth thou springest
> Like a cloud of fire;

The deep blue thou wingest,
And singing still dost soar, and soaring ever singest...

Every true poem represents either the momentary dominance of one rhythm — which is ecstasy; or the meeting and incorporating of different rhythms of experience in an individual, in varying degrees of conflict; or the tranquil movement of restored balance, imperceptibly echoing an earlier conflict. Wherever you catch emotion alive, there can be no absolutely regular rhythm.

A poem is rather like a sample cut for you at the ribbon counter: an especially significant bit of human experience snipped off to show you its color and texture. The poet does this by his choice and arrangement of words, and he would have a difficult time if his own rhythms and habits of associating one thing with another did not direct him with little nudges and pokings all along the way. He has also a knowledge of the various ways other poets have said things; he can diagram their rhythms and verse patterns; but once you take these patterns away from the substance that informed them, they mean very little. Their value lies only in their fitness.

Regular English verse depends upon the principle of contrasting accents, but it has always employed the metres of Greek and Latin poetry, the classic metres, as a measuring-rule. Greek and Latin poetry depended upon the principle of contrasting weights — the sounds of their syllables actually lasted longer; people danced to them. English verse measures off most naturally into groups of two and groups of three syllables. These pairs and triplets are called *feet*.

Two-syllable feet have an accent either on the first or the last syllable called the *strong* or *long* or *heavy* syllable. The other syllable is called *short* or *light*.

When the first syllable is light, the second heavy, the foot is iambic:

I won|der what|it's all|about

When the first syllable is heavy, the second light, the foot is trochaic:

Wonder|not a|bout the|reason

Three-syllable feet have either the first or last syllable accented. The other two are light.

A three-syllable foot with the accent on the last syllable is anapestic:

How I won|der whatev|er this thing|is about

A three-syllable foot with the accent on the first syllable is dactylic:

Wondering|what it is|ever a|bout

Lines of verse contain from one to seven or eight feet, though when they reach that length, their meaning generally causes them to break in two and they are best considered as two shorter lines.

Very few lines of poetry are composed entirely of one kind of foot. One metre predominates, but feeling and meaning will cause variations and pauses. Sometimes there are pauses where a light syllable would otherwise occur. This often happens at the beginnings and ends of lines. Sometimes the emphasis will reverse a foot, substituting a trochee for an iamb, or light syllables creep in and your trochee or iamb stretches out into a dactyl or an anapest, giving a little run and skip to the metre. These help to make a line flexible and musical, while pauses or rests give that haunting quality, that charm, paralleled by syncopation in music.

Sidney Lanier experimented in measuring verse by musical notation, but this proved uselessly complicated. The habit of counting one's syllables — so many to a line as if they were all of equal stress — is a poor method, since the most important thing in the case of regular lines is to have the same number of strong accents in a line. Reading aloud is the one sure test for sound and fundamental rhythm, though we must guard against the tendency, when reading our own work, to slur over certain accents and emphasize others in order to make the line come right. Read your lines aloud many times; mark the accents and count them; and then make sure that their meaning flows directly and sinuously. The stresses of actual speech are exactly what no mechanical scheme of syllables can take into account. The only way to become skilled in handling them is to listen for them everywhere; to remember expressions and accents of genuinely stirred emotion. You will not forget them if you have responded to them.

When you read Robert Frost's poetry, you will discover that the words are so framed that they can be spoken with only one emphasis. The words themselves are generally simple to the point of commonplaceness, but their arrangement is unique. He knows where the accents of feeling lodge in everyday phrases and has placed his words with such precision that the feeling is unmistakable. Our voices assume it inevitably because the regularity of his lines is dedicated entirely to his thought.

> I think the little fellow's afraid of the snow.
> He isn't winter-broken. It isn't play
> With the little fellow at all. He's running away.
> I doubt if even his mother could tell him, 'Sakes,
> It's only weather! He'd think she didn't know!...
> Whoever it is that leaves him out so late
> When other creatures have gone to stall and bin,
> Ought to be told to come and take him in.
>
> ('The Runaway.')

For some time people have felt that the old verse patterns were inadequate to express rhythms that they recognized in life and found beautiful, and they have experimented, avoiding rhyme and regular lines, depending more upon speech cadence and the longer rhythms of prose, writing something they called free verse. Actually, free verse has been in existence for many centuries. Prose translations of the earliest Greek and Chinese poetry — intrinsically poetic ideas simply and economically worded — are really free verse. The prophetic books of the Bible, the choruses to Milton's 'Samson Agonistes,' are free verse. Matthew Arnold, W. E. Henley, and Francis Thompson occasionally wrote free verse. In America Walt Whitman was the first to make this departure. He said, in explanation: 'As I have lived in fresh lands, inchoate, and in a revolutionary age, future-founding, I have felt to identify the points of that age, these lands, in my recitatives, altogether in my own way. Thus my form has strictly grown from my purports and facts and is the analogy of them.'

Just what are the differences between prose and free verse? Direct prose statements are like messages over the telephone — nothing matters but the news that is transmitted. But everything about poetry is news: the sound of it, the beat of it, the words that are chosen as best capable of conveying the message — words that perhaps never met before, and are now united in the close fraternity of a common purpose. Words so put together will never have the slipshod step of careless speech. They make use of the power and beauty latent in common speech, but they leave out what is dull and long-winded and inaccurate. So employed they are not common, they have the bearing of people engaged upon a great mission.

Often in prose writing we find passages, winged with feeling and shapely with compact meaning. These, except for the way they happen to be printed upon the page, are poetry — free verse. Thoreau wrote as prose in his journal on the fifteenth of June, 1852:

It is candle light.
The fishes leap,
The meadows sparkle with the coppery light of fire-flies.
The evening star
Multiplied by undulating water,
Is like bright sparks of fire continually ascending.

Here, in a free verse arrangement, the natural pauses occasioned by the sequence of thought determine when a new line shall begin.

The cadences of free verse differ from prose rhythms in their tenseness, their wiriness. They are accelerated by stronger feeling. Often, in a wider range than that of regular verse, they repeat themselves, the unity of the poet's thought taking again and again the same pattern. There are fewer words used in free verse than in a prose statement of the same idea, a concentration resulting naturally from the crystallization of thought and feeling.

If a poem is a revelation of the poet's nature, then free verse is a 'dead give-away.' There is no hiding behind the palings of regular lines, no kind obscurities of epithet or thick-leaved simile, no verse form to tell you where to leave off. It is your idea which must have a beginning and a conclusion if there is to be a poem; it is your feeling which must have condensed into clear imagery; it is the actual harmony or disharmony of your nature which directs the beat of your words in original rhythms — rhythms native to the particular thought and feeling which caused the poem. Of course, much of the free verse which we read is not like this, but is it good poetry?

Free verse is neither better nor worse than regular verse. The better poetry is that where the form and the thought flow together like two streams mingled in the channel of the poet's nature. There are certain short poems, T. E. Brown's 'Vespers,' for example, where the idea and

the form are inseparable, and rhyme has turned
the key on them:

> O blackbird, what a boy you are!
> How you do go it!
> Blowing your bugle to that one sweet star —
> How you do blow it!
> And does she hear you, blackbird boy, so far?
> Or is it wasted breath?
> 'Good Lord! she is so bright
> Tonight!'
> The blackbird saith.

All American Indian poems are songs, and an
Indian was once asked which came first, the words
or the music. 'They come together,' he replied.
That is the natural way for poetry to come: a
completely conceived idea taking shape in words
and rhythms which are of its nature, the form
being a record of natural growth. Emerson wrote:
'It is not metres but a metre-making argument
that makes a poem — a thought so passionate and
alive that, like the spirit of a plant or an animal,
it has an architecture of its own, and adorns nature
with a new thing.'

IV

SOUND

Sound is the primitive medium by which most of the higher animals both express and excite emotion; and hence, though until codified into human speech it does not give any raw material for art, yet so powerful are its primitive effects that music (in the birdsong sense of sound indulged in for its own attractiveness) is as long prior to language as the brilliant colours of animals and flowers are prior to painting.

The Encyclopædia Britannica

UNLESS we are very much preoccupied, we rarely hear a sound without unconsciously determining its source. 'Somebody must have dropped a pan in the kitchen.' 'That is the postman's ring.' We have an enormous catalogue of sounds filed away in our memories. What is more sharply suggestive than the whirr of the first lawn-mower in spring, or the creak of icy wheels early in the morning telling us that the thermometer has dropped to zero? Babies distinguish sounds before they recognize words. They know anger and indulgence in the human voice; they identify the bark of a dog, a rooster's crow, and try to imitate them. If you sit quietly in the woods some summer day, its great stillness gradually becomes full of sound: infinite small sounds of wind and leaves, of water, of insects and birds, of twigs dropping to the ground, the traffic and industry of chipmunks, moles, and field mice. These sounds, though you may not hear them often enough to identify them instantly when you hear them somewhere else, are yet tabulated in your memory along with quietness, summer woods, perhaps some personal relationship — everything that happened on that holiday to make you feel it deeply and so record it enduringly within your consciousness.

It is this habit of association that the musician and the poet play upon when they recall to you a few of the great accumulation of natural sounds which are common to nearly everyone's experience. Modern musicians are introducing mechanical sounds, city sounds, into their compositions in the quickened nervous rhythms of present-day living, causing fresh excitement in their hearers. Sound, harmonized to his mood and related to his meaning, can help the poet to convey his 'felt thought' to the very heart of his reader, for while the meaning of his words is being perceived intellectually, their sound has already made a more direct contact with the reader's memory-charged emotions, provoking an involuntary response.

Robert Frost once said: 'What I have been after from the first, consciously and unconsciously, is tones of voice. I've wanted to write down certain brute throat noises so that no one could miss them in my sentences. I have been guilty of speaking of sentences as a mere notation for indicating them. They have been my observation and my subject-matter.' The human voice was our first musical instrument, and its tones have naturally a greater suggestive power than any other sounds. They have the same immediate effect upon us that muscular images have because they are actually caused by sudden tenseness in the muscles of the throat, sharp emotional contractions, quick warmth and depths of tone coming from an expansion of the whole personality. One often hears a human voice shouting or crying out in Robinson Jeffers's poetry. In the first stanza of his 'Noon,' the long *a*'s and the wide intervals of sound give the effect of a voice issuing from an open throat:

> The pure air trembles, O pitiless God,
> The air aches with flame on these gaunt rocks
> Over the flat sea's face, the forest
> Shakes in gales of piercing light.

Free sound, we do not have in speech, but we have a wide scale of tones in the vowel sounds of words; and notes of different duration. A scale of vowel sounds can be made somewhat like a musical scale:

> Oh, oo, aw, ah, ite, at, et, it, ate, eet.

The positions of the sounds in this scale are, I must add, open to dispute, since each person's voice will give them different values.

Broad harmonies of sound, comparable to wide intervals in music, are found in themes that have size, swiftness, and intensity. Close harmonies consistent with small detail, a shorter step, a muted voice, the *o*'s of bated breath, are in Emily Dickinson's

> I know some lonely houses off the road
> A robber'd like the look of —
> Wooden barred,
> And windows hanging low
> Inviting to
> A portico...

Fortunately for the poet, a great number of words sound like the thing or the action they name — onomatopoetic words. Many of them must have been invented to describe their object or act as naturally as a baby calls a dog a bow-wow.

Some of our words have sounds unrelated to and more beautiful than their meaning: *cellar door*, for instance, which a cultured Chinaman thought the most beautiful word in the English language. Its beauty had to be pointed out to us, the users of the language, because we perceive its meaning consciously, its sound unconsciously, and, of course,

the meaning is more important, for communication.
Swinburne was more concerned with the sound
of his words than their meaning:

The sound of a word was shed, the sound of the wind as
a breath,
In the ears of the souls that were dead, in the dust of the
deepness of death;
When the face of the moon is taken, the ways of the
stars undone,
The light of the whole sky shaken, the light of the face
of the sun....

('A Song in Time of Revolution.')

He often spread his meaning very thin. Poe, except
on a few occasions, used sound with mechanical
rather than organic accuracy. Carl Sandburg has a
keen ear for lovely monotones:

Stuff of the moon
Runs on the lapping sand
Out to the longest shadows.
Under the curving willows,
And round the creep of the wave line,
Fluxions of yellow dusk on the waters
Make a wide dreaming pansy of an old pond in the
night.

('Nocturne in a Deserted Brickyard.')

Elinor Wylie has woven matchless harmonies in her
'Hymn to Earth':

Farewell, incomparable element,
Whence man arose, where he shall not return;
And hail, imperfect urn
Of his last ashes, and his firstborn fruit;
Farewell, the long pursuit,
And all the adventures of his discontent;
The voyages which sent
His heart averse from home:
Metal of clay, permit him that he come
To thy slow-burning fire as to a hearth;
Accept him as a particle of earth.

Harmonies of vowel sounds are, of course, not complete without music between the consonants which enclose them. In speech certain consonants follow one another easily, such as the liquid *l*'s and *r*'s, *m*'s and *n*'s. Some consonants — *p*, *b*, *d*, *t* — close the lips at the end of a word and force a pause. A line filled with *s* sounds hisses in our ears.

The repetition of consonants in a line is called alliteration. 'In the dust of the deepness of death' is an example. A little of it goes a long way. It should be almost imperceptible, stroked in lightly among the unaccented syllables, widely spaced. Alliteration is a fairly unconscious habit with those who delight in words. You will probably weed it out in revising your work oftener than you will consciously employ it. It lends a decided emphasis to strong syllables.

The first recorded poem that we have in earliest English, Cædmon's 'Hymn,' has a pattern of sounds; repeated vowels and consonants in accented syllables emphasizing the rough bumping metre of the lines:

Nū wē sculon *h*erigan *h*eofonrīces Weard	H
*M*eotodes *m*eahte ond his *m*ōdgethanc	M
*W*eorc *W*oldorfaeder swā hē *w*undra geh*w*aes	W
Ēce Drihten ōr onstealde	O

Rhyme is the repetition of joined vowel and consonant sounds. It delights us in various ways: by the mere pleasure of repeated sounds and by the sense it gives us of difficulty overcome. When two words are rhymed, something has happened; eventfulness is added to the poem. Rhymes put knots in the ends of our lines, drawing the meaning snug, or joining them smoothly together. Easy familiar pairs of rhymes — *years* and *tears*, *trees* and *breeze*, *sorrow* and *tomorrow*, *love* and *dove* — are about as obvious and unbeautiful as hooks-and-eyes. But the unexpected rhyme, that pleases both by its inventiveness and its naturalness, is as graceful as a well-tied knot.

Now it is a simple matter to lay out the first lines of a poem. In a quatrain, for example, the first rhyme is comparatively easy because the end of your thought is still waving loose. But with one knot made, the direction of your words has been somewhat determined and the second knot, the final rhyme, is the more difficult. We often go around this difficulty by putting a new sentence or a clause in the last line, but you will discover, if you watch, that the best rhymed poetry allows few such makeshifts. The writers realized that they were rhyming sentences, not words, and they constructed their verses so that the thought flows with superlative ease and compactness in the last lines of stanzas, the fourth and eighth lines of sonnets, and always the last line of any poem. Their final rhyme is like the lash on the end of a whip.

Words do not have to be spelled alike to rhyme, but they must sound alike. Words which would rhyme, if one of them did not have a plural *s* (*rooms — tomb*) are not considered true rhymes; nor are words with the same vowel sound, but *n* and *m* for ending consonants (*time — dine*). Words which are entirely alike in sound, though not in spelling (*bare — bear*), are called identical rhymes, and should be avoided. Sometimes a writer will deliberately use an imperfect rhyme where the end consonants are alike, but the vowels are slightly different in tone (such as *earth* and *hearth* in the 'Hymn to Earth' just quoted), because he wants the shadowy effect sounds have when they merely echo each other. Emily Dickinson often does this, whether from choice or through the inevitableness of her imagery, we can hardly tell.

One-syllable rhymes are called masculine and have generally more force and less grace than feminine two-syllable rhymes. Two-syllable rhymes alternating with shorter rhymes add delicacy and movement, as in Sidney's love song:

> 'Who is it that this dark night
>   Underneath my window plaineth?'
> It is one who from thy sight
>   Being, ah, exiled, disdaineth
> Every other vulgar light.

Intricate rhymes and three-syllable rhyme schemes are used chiefly in witty and satiric poetry. Rhymes of such length are conspicuous. In serious poetry it is difficult to employ them without startling and distracting the reader from the sustained and single mood intended by the poet.

All sorts of uses may be made of rhyme, though it is ordinarily not employed in free verse. Wherever it is used, it must happen often enough to arouse our expectation and then gratify it. Sometimes rhymes are scattered irregularly throughout a poem within the lines; occasionally they are put at the beginning of lines, but neither arrangement helps a direct forward movement of thought. Prob-

ably there are new uses for rhyme not yet discovered, but the essential nature of it is this: an
echoing of sound which tends to make the reader
pause for enjoyment and possibly think back. It
gives a sense of termination, of something having
happened.

Sound is somewhat at a discount in modern poetry because we read mostly to ourselves, silently.
Words are used whose sounds are inharmonious.
Sometimes diction depends upon punctuation for
intelligibility of statement; the very pattern of type
upon a page is used for certain effects. But words,
rhythm, and sound are the poet's especial province,
and the artist is wise to stay within his own medium.
A modern poet, Archibald MacLeish, uses sound
and rhythm so skillfully to accentuate his meaning
that he needs hardly any punctuation.

Our history is grave noble and tragic
We trusted the look of the sun on the green leaves
We built our towns of stone with enduring ornaments
We worked the hard flint for basins of water
                                        ('Men.')

Musicians are able to hear tones in imagination
as they think of them. Poets need this faculty also
and can develop it by reading their lines and verses
aloud as they work over them, testing them for the

right quality of sound. But to a certain extent, just as we perceive sound unconsciously, we recall and reproduce it unconsciously. When we concentrate upon an idea, turning it around in our imaginations, the sounds and rhythms that belong with it by nature are recalled into consciousness, suggesting words to us. Sometimes it is not the right word. Often it is a word bordering on the right meaning, or even a word with the right sound but the wrong meaning. We have to hold fast to our purpose, looking up synonyms in the dictionary, trying and rejecting words until we find those which say exactly what we intend, with native harmony. Always, the poetic conception should ride the words, guiding their direction, ruling their pace.

V

FORM

Substance engenders form exactly as the tortoise or the oyster do the materials of their respective shells.

REMY DE GOURMONT

ONE of the first men to foresee the revolution in architecture if tall structures of steel and concrete were to take the place of stone and wooden buildings — Louis Sullivan — took as his creed: 'Function determines form.' When he had plans to draw for a new building, he asked himself first for what the building was to be used and where it was to stand. His conception for the building drew its vitality from this basic idea of the true meaning of the building and its surroundings. His conviction brought into existence entirely new ideas about the proportions of buildings, the materials of which they were constructed, the ornament which adorned them.

Nowadays, the mere fitness of a thing seems to many of us sufficient ornament. The steel tool, completely adapted to its function and finely finished, is as beautiful to us as the highly ornamented antique sword with its jeweled hilt. Writers have the same feeling about form and ornament in poetry. They admire more the poetry, which is merely an emotion completed in thought and put in terms of its natural environment, than a poem whose lines are encrusted heavily with jeweled words. The impulse to adorn, to display, is no longer foremost.

This implies, of course, a very clear idea of what you want to say, and a confidence, based upon experience, in your capacity to set that idea free; to allow it to emerge of itself as reverently as flowers are permitted to open and butterflies to take their strange instinctive way out of their cocoons. It is as if you said to that idea beating its wings in your breast: 'Take your own way out, and I will help all I can.' This is really not so difficult because it is natural for us to have ideas and give them free utterance.

Imagine a young Arab who has never known how to read or write. He loves a girl and so she seems beautiful to him. When he thinks of her beauty, other things which have seemed beautiful also come into his mind. He is happy in thinking of her so that he hums to himself, and his thoughts go along with his humming, perhaps like this:

> Fourteen thy days, O lovely moon at full;
> Fourteen the years of my gazelle-eyed love;
> Yet brighter far her face, more beautiful.

Two red lips hast thou not, O moon above,
Thou hast not teeth like whitest pearl arrayed
Nor braided plaits like those which deck my love.
                    (FULANIAN, 'The Marsh Arab.')

The fourteen days of the moon brought to the
lover's mind the fourteen years of his love. Com-
paring her to the moon gave him an opportunity to
count over her especial charms, and the thought
patterned out into two parallel three-line stanzas.
Probably they were rhymed in Arabic, since rhyme
has long been practiced by the Chinese, the Per-
sians, and the Arabs.

One can hardly give an exclamation without
making a start toward a verse form. I say exclamation because such remarks have the impulse of
emotion. Even if you have never tried to write a
line of poetry, you have spoken words under the
influence of feeling that could have been lines in a
poem. Your feeling found the words. But something more is needed. The thought that like a
current of electricity caused a chemical reaction
between the Arab's dream of his love and the
moon's appearance was that these two, so different
in many characteristics, had fourteen of their
particular units in common. He found the full
moon an appropriate image for the thought which
was uppermost in his mind, the beauty of the girl
he loved.

Have you ever noticed how you will catch your-self some bright morning singing an old song you have not thought of in years; and how a dismal long-forgotten hymn will come to mind another day? They fitted your mood with their gay or mournful cadences and so they were unconsciously selected by you from your store of recollections. Certain kinds of activities: riding, rowing, skating, and dancing will bring various tunes to mind be-cause the rhythms fit; and because our songs, in turn, grew out of these living metres. Weavers, in the days of hand-looms, were famous for their singing, the even lengths of their thread setting the time perfectly for their voices. Often words will come to you in a short sentence or phrase having a definite rhythm to express a mood, an experience, or an idea, and these words are likely ultimately to be your first or last line and will suggest the rhythm of the whole poem.

Do not substitute other words hastily for the words which first occurred to you, just to make them fit a certain verse form. Those particular words may say exactly what you mean and be the making of a new and harmonious form. Suppose a poem begins with a verse of four lines, a quatrain. You might continue with that stanza form to the end of the poem. But often that will be inconsistent with the development of your thought, and the end of the poem is feeble. Without the stanza form, the unity of your idea might still have given your words shapeliness and the poem might have been shorter, more compact and individual. Sometimes a verse form is set up like a trellis and sprawling vines of thought are looped over it. The writer of that poem merely encouraged a weakness in his thinking.

Often the polishing that poets put upon their lines is only a process of removing the uninspired words they first inserted to carry out the verse scheme, and recalling with difficulty the original emotion which caused the poem in order to find more vital expressions.

Rightly employed, a verse form may lead you to explore the full possibilities of your idea. Sea-gulls, when they take flight from the water, always rise against the wind, finding a support for their mounting in its opposition. So the beat of a definite verse form opposed to his thought has helped to launch many a poet's idea. But after the gulls' wings find their beat, have you noticed how quickly they turn and go *with* the wind?

The various forms in which poetry has been cast since its beginnings all first came into being as the shape of some insistent germ of thought and feeling. From what have these forms taken their natures? What do they do best?

Tracing the origin of certain French lyric forms, Miss Helen Louise Cohen writes: 'If we judge from the analogy of other primitive peoples, it is very certain that sophisticated and artistic poetic forms, like the ballade and rondel, which employ a regular refrain, are in the direct line of a long descent from choral folk-songs, in which the people of the village coöperated with an accomplished leader in raising the dance-song which accompanied their movements.'

The ballade, the chant royal, the rondel or rondeau, the villanelle, the triolet, are all poems with refrains more or less intricate in their arrangement of rhymes. In the days when verse-writing was the polite accomplishment of every courtier in France and Italy, these forms were especially popular. Being able to write a neat rondel or ballade was equivalent to playing a good hand of bridge today. It was a game. But 'playing and creative activities are essentially opposed,' according to Mr. Leo Stein. 'Creation is the making of something, and the thing to be made is the only intrinsic term'; in other words, the one thing to be considered. Many of the ballades and villanelles and triolets which have been written are like designs in a piece of lace or a much-repeated pattern in wood-carving, a conventionalized figure in a piece of damask. The design dominates the substance and wins most of

our admiration. Such forms serve best in giving
shape to wit and satire, regret, pathos, and com-
pliments.

This is not always so. There is not much forward movement in forms with repeated rhymes and
refrains, forms derived from dance measures. Swift
emotions are out of place in forms which move in a
circle. But this very repetition helps to sustain a
mood, and Chaucer, Villon, and Swinburne had the
richness of mood, the intellectual wealth and the
skill to brim their ballades and rondeaus with un-
diluted poetry. It is a point worth noticing that
when the significant characteristics of a close verse
pattern can be used to enhance the poet's meaning,
the poem gains by being cast in that form. His sea-
gull, in other words, has reached the upper air and
is riding with the wind.

The triolet, a little eight-line stanza with only
two rhymes and several lines repeated, has been
chiefly used for gayety and pathos or for invective.
But in this triolet by Adelaide Crapsey a great
weight of feeling is carried with the lightness of
perfect balance:

> I make my shroud but no one knows —
> So shimmering fine it is and fair,
> With stitches set in even rows.
> I make my shroud but no one knows.
> In door-ways where the lilac blows,

Humming a little wandering air,
I make my shroud and no one knows,
So shimmering fine it is and fair.

François Villon employed an abbreviated rondeau with a single-syllabled refrain to carry a live burden of grief. Dante Gabriel Rossetti translated it in these lines:

To Death, of His Lady

Death, of thee do I make my moan,
Who hadst my lady away from me,
Nor wilt assuage thine enmity
Till with her life thou hast mine own.
For since that hour my strength has flown.
Lo! What wrong was her life to thee,
    Death?

Two we were, and the heart was one;
Which now being dead, dead I must be,
Or seem alive as lifelessly
As in the choir the painted stone,
    Death!

So verse forms and rhyme schemes may seem iron in their inflexibility and yet bend, when they are selected, perhaps inexplicably, by the poet brooding over his material, and brought near the white heat of his thought. The proof will lie in the apparent naturalness of this fusion of idea and

form. If the result seems labored, the poem fails.
It has no happy adequacy.

The sonnet is a fixed form of fourteen lines with
a variety of rhyme scheme, and yet it seems to fit
the pattern of a developing thought so well that it
is used over and over again with fresh effect. The
Italian sonnet has two parts: an octet of eight lines
followed by a sestet of six — just enough room, ap-
parently, for expanding that germ of poetry — the
discovery of a likeness between something outside
the poet and something inside him. Shakespeare
patterned his thought a little differently in his sonnets — three four-line stanzas more loosely rhymed
than the Italian, in which his thought moved
swiftly forward to a concluding couplet. The close
rhyme locked his idea in with a culminating
snap.

In many sonnets the last six lines begin with an
outburst of personal feeling. In some a climax is
reached on the last line. The form accommodates
all sorts of emotions. There are stately sonnets,
passionate sonnets, playful, spiteful, teasing sonnets. In some of the best you will notice that the
poet said all he had to say in twelve or thirteen
lines; the other line or two are just padding.

Generally a sonnet is composed of five-foot
(iambic pentameter) lines, but lines of shorter or

longer length have been used, and variations played upon the rhyme scheme. Usually the lines are of the same length, but in her 'Sonnets from an Ungrafted Tree' Edna St. Vincent Millay has closed her iambic pentameter sonnets with a six-foot line. When the rhymes come closer together, the thought progression seems more rapid. When we must wait longer to hear a sound re-occur, the movement is slower, more rhythmical. The individual quality of your thought, at grips with a fixed form, may even cause a new arrangement of lines and rhymes which will become a new sonnet form.

Stanza forms accommodate themselves more easily than these forms which are complete units, and they permit greater freedom in patterning your thought. What will not go into one stanza laps over into the next, and we often see a group of stanzas where part of a sentence is carried over from stanza to stanza. If you make the fullest use of a verse form, however, you will let your meaning profit by the concluding effect each separate verse possesses.

Long stanzas, long lines, and irregular rhyme-schemes lend themselves well to dreamy, meditative moods. Do you know the rich stanzas of Spenser's 'Faerie Queene,' or those of Matthew Arnold's 'Scholar Gipsy'?

In autumn, on the skirts of Bagley-wood,
Where most the gipsies by the turf-edged way
Pitch their smoked tents, and every bush you see
With scarlet patches tagged, and shreds of gray,
Above the forest-ground called Thessaly —
The blackbird picking food
Sees thee, nor stops his meal, nor fears at all!
So often has he known thee past him stray
Rapt, twirling in thy hand a withered spray,
And waiting for the spark from Heaven to fall.

Five-line stanzas hold a little more element of surprise in their arrangement, a little greater variety in their rhyme-schemes, than four-line stanzas.

Stanzas of three lines, all rhyming, or rhyming occasionally, maintain a slow, circling rhythm that carries an echo of waltz time.

Four-line stanzas of four- and three-foot lines rhyming alternately are called ballad metre, so many of the old rhymed ballads were told in this verse form. The short statements and descriptive phrases which constitute stories fall easily into three- and four-foot lines. The alternating rhymes keep pointing the reader to the future; he knows what the end of the fourth line is going to sound like when he has heard the second. The rhymes and the action of the story seem to move forward hand in hand.

'Make haste, make haste, my merry men all,
  Our good ship sails the morn:'
'O say not so, my master dear,
  For I fear a deadly storm.'

'Late, late yestreen, I saw the new moon
  With the old moon in her arm,
And I fear, I fear, my dear master,
  That we will come to harm.'
(From 'Sir Patrick Spence.')

Couplets (two-line verses) encourage short, pithy statements, clever, neat sayings; and the close rhymes make the reader pause long enough to savor their full meaning. Alexander Pope (noted for his wit) used them so well that his name will always be associated with them.

Blank verse consisting of five-foot iambic lines is the accepted measure for long poems in English verse. Rhyme is likely to become monotonous after a page or so. Blank verse is the nearest thing we have in measured verse to ordinary speech; often people fall into it unconsciously when they talk. It seems to fit our breathing. Perhaps there is a connection between the naturalness of blank verse and the fact that we are used to counting fives on our fingers.

Blank verse is a measure that allows the user rope enough to hang himself. There is nothing but his own judgment, his poetic purpose, to prevent him from filling innumerable lines with prosy utterances. But it also allows him opportunity for large effects, or for a beautiful simplicity. Shakespeare's plays, Milton's 'Paradise Lost,' give indications of its range. Do you recall how, after all the thunder and glory of Heaven and Hell, Adam and Eve departed from Paradise?

Some natural tears they dropped, but wiped them soon;
The world was all before them, where to choose
Their place of rest, and Providence their guide.
They, hand in hand, with wandering steps and slow
Through Eden took their solitary way.

In this country and these times Edwin Arlington Robinson and Robert Frost have employed blank verse in new ways, because they see life in new terms, and so poets will continue to do down the ages, investing old forms with fresh vitality or creating new units of rhythm to carry their ideas, to shape their poems.

What is a poem, anyhow? The shortest poem in the world would have to have more than two words in it and at least two lines, for it is something made, put together of component elements. Once made, it should have the unity, the bare-essential quality of created things. As Archibald MacLeish says in his 'Ars Poetica':

A poem should not mean
But be.

It should not describe or tell, it should suggest and awaken, through any thought and feeling possible to human minds, a sharp consciousness of life. Whether it is two lines long, four lines, eight or fourteen or a hundred — and Poe has said that there are no long poems, meaning that no true poem is very long — it should be an entity as separate as a dog or a flower or a human being. Its form and content should be as closely related as flesh and bone. For with poetry as with architecture or the human anatomy, 'Function determines form.'

VI

THE ARTIST

In every human being there is the artist, and whatever his activity, he has an equal chance with any to express the result of his growth and his contact with life.... I don't believe any real artist cares whether what he does is 'art' or not. Who, after all, knows what is art? I think the real artists are too busy with just being and growing and acting (on canvas or however) like themselves, to worry about the end. The end will be what it will be. The object is intense living, fulfillment, the great happiness in creation.

ROBERT HENRI

It is interesting that a book of unrelated comments and criticisms, made by Robert Henri to his art students, should contain much that is applicable to writing. But it is natural enough. The same principles underlie all expression. We used to think that poets were born, not made, and that if they had this impulse, nothing could stop them from being poets. But some of the most beautiful poems we have, some of the loveliest songs, happened into the world simply because a person who had no intention of being a great poet experienced joy or sorrow deeply, and eased his heart by putting that feeling into words. Perhaps he merely wanted to please someone he loved, and made the song as another man might carve something of wood, or gather certain flowers that looked beautiful together. Perhaps, as Rebecca West suggests, he was interpreting his experience to himself. But always, whatever the occasion, there was the underlying desire for expression, to release a discovery too beautiful, too poignant, to keep to one's self.

Now beauty is not a precious element, a static substance which can be isolated. It consists in the *way* things are put together and react upon each other. Happiness is the consciousness of harmony, balance, and, above all, adequacy; and art gives us this happiness through representations of these principles in all sorts of terms. 'Here is God's plenty!' exclaimed Dryden, speaking of Chaucer's poetry.

We derive a sense of well-being and pleasure from the proportion and balance and adequacy of our bodies when we are in good health. That, too, is beauty. A machine has beauty when it fulfills its purpose with easy power. In a tragedy it may be only the fulfilling of a natural law, terrible in its consequences, which can be called beautiful. But wherever this element of adequate natural functioning in relation to environment is found, there beauty is — in a life, in an emotion, in a landscape, in a ship or a tool or a piece of furniture. To all of us some of its aspects will mean nothing, because of the limitations of our experience, but beauty is there, in equations which are clear and true to anyone who understands the terms. Robert Frost once said: 'I hope I have some range in the appreciation of beauty. I can see it all the way from exquisite through homely and mean, even to vile.'

One might say that poetry is a quality of intense and loving vision which finds expression in words. Padraic Colum has called it 'the discovery of the uniqueness in things.' In a poem the rhythms and suggestive power of the words invoke some piece of human experience so well that it is alive for us — 'big as life and twice as handsome,' in the old phrase — because the poet has selected parts of the experience to tell us, choosing the unifying factors with so wise an instinct that we seem to have the whole experience — simplified. To give this selective faculty the right chance, we must remove from our consciousness the silt and twigs and dried leaves of our preconceived notions of how one goes about being a poet. The spring is there, and if we wait, the water will come clear. Technique is the cup with which we dip up poetry. Some people use their bare palms, but even they have a knack, to keep the water from slipping back through their fingers.

Whether you become a great poet or writer depends much upon the soundness of your desire to write, and upon your ability to recognize greatness in your own living and in the life of your own times.

It depends upon whether you experience completely for poetry is, after all, nothing but realized experience put in communicable terms. It depends a great deal upon your power of concentration. It will be proved, perhaps, many years after fame has become of no importance to you, but with your fellow artists, you will have given tangible evidence 'that perfect bright experience never falls to nothingness.'

Wanting to be a poet may be only an indication that you are afraid to take hold of life as most people live it. You may be using that ambition as a convenient lever to pry you loose from conditions of living that you hate, a piece of personal adornment to compensate for the fact that you do not seem especially desirable to others. In such cases, with a change of circumstance, your ambition to write will die. Another flaw in your purpose may lie in wanting to be a certain kind of person instead of wanting to do a certain kind of thing — to be a poet rather than to write poetry. That is like choosing a job for the uniform. Even loving poetry may mean only that you like to read it, not write it.

But if you have a genuine capacity to manage words, it is your writing, rather than a mere desire to write, which will persist in spite of obstacles and distractions. And these last will grow less as you build your life around that main purpose, relating every factor to it. Then, whatever happens, whatever is within your line of vision, has value for you and the treasure is stored away. Sooner or later you will draw upon it.

Walt Whitman, in an apostrophe to the past, concludes:

> I stand in my place with my own day here.

You lose an inheritance when you ignore the past. You can learn much from the work of great poets, especially from observing how and why they wrought in that fashion. But none of them ever copied except as a trial of skill. Each one of them, too, stood in his place with his own day there.

Where is that place? Thoreau wrote in his journal on the twentieth of November, 1857: 'A man is worth most to himself and to others, whether as an observer, a poet, or neighbor, or friend, who is most contented and at home. There his life is the most intense and he loses the fewest moments. Familiar and surrounding objects are the best symbols and illustrations of his life.... Here I have been these forty years learning the language of these fields that I may the better express myself. If I should travel on the prairies, I should much less understand them, and my past life would serve me but ill to describe them. Many a weed stands for more of life to me than the big trees of California would, if I should go there.'

'With my own day here.' You have a certain length of time in which to share your life with those who happen to be alive upon the earth when you are. Your words and thoughts will mean more to your contemporaries than they ever can convey, however immortal, to future generations. You may be more admired and appreciated then, but you can never have the opportunity later of being so completely comprehended — of making a perfect communication. The values of words change, our conceptions change, science changes our world. Your writing will take on new colors, lovely, perhaps, but not those you intended. This alone is sufficient reason for writing with your heart in the present and writing to publish.

Poets are not often able to support themselves by their art, but many a one has scaled his living down to a simplicity which allows him to write more and better poetry. Like all the best things of life, poetry cannot actually be bought or sold. It has its own rewards. And it deserves that you should be diligent in your efforts to find it an audience through print.

No one can teach you to write poetry. But having learned to look for it, you can train yourself to record it with all the skill of which you are capable.

It is useless to keep your hand on your own pulse, waiting for a throb to manufacture into poetry. What you write under such circumstances will not be poetry because it expresses no true response; it springs from a forced, unreal situation. Nor do you need to lead a life particularly free from ordinary restraints. Only by participating in life in its most ordinary ways can you learn to interpret and re-create it. But you must have free time to practice your art, and until you are past the first years of your apprenticeship, such time is hard to secure. Ordinarily the young artist takes it from his hours of recreation — in fact, it becomes his recreation. He develops the thrifty habit of seeing possibilities for poetry in his studies, in his most casual observations as he walks along the street, in his associations with other people.

I know an artist who never goes out of his way for subjects to paint. He makes his living in a litho-graphing establishment, and in his free time he sketches his dooryard, a bit of the road in front of his house, the view from his barn door, the children who love to visit his studio; and every sketch is a fresh aspect, a new discovery of these familiar things. His paintings are exhibited all over the country; they take many prizes, and his con-temporaries say that he has mastered line. He said to me recently: 'Here is something I read that will help you — "the greatest art is in the accidental meetings."'

Those illuminating accidental meetings between your feeling self and your environment when you suddenly see a part of your experience in homely terms — those are times of inspiration. Art does this. It relates you to your environment so that you draw directly from the earth beneath your feet that nourishment for mind and soul, without which no nature thrives. When you can create beauty in any form out of your environment, it is as if you struck root as a tree does wherever it happens to be planted, and began sending out new branches every year, sweet with flowers, heavy with fruit.

POEMS BY MEMBERS OF THE
STEVENSON ROOM POETRY GROUP
OF THE
CLEVELAND PUBLIC LIBRARY

POEMS BY MEMBERS OF THE
STEVENSON ROOM POETRY GROUP
OF THE
CLEVELAND PUBLIC LIBRARY

. .

STAIRWAYS

SOME people like to have
long stairways so that they may
strut upon them slowly and,
gracefully as peacocks, look down
as they walk up higher... higher.

Others want long stairways so
that they can leap upwards
taking four or five steps to a
stride not caring how they go —
they carelessly shoot up... up.

I want a long stairway too,
a long winding stairway,
one that reaches way up high —
so that I may slowly tread up, and
watch my shadow thrown

upon the wall unproportionately,
and walk when no one is around...
laugh at my grey comrade on the wall,
and bawl him out,
and tell him where to get off.

I want a long stairway,
so that I will have a long walk
before I reach the top —
so that I can walk up slowly,
one by one
watching my shadow
walking with me.

HERMAN ABROMSON. Aged 20.

CURIOSITY

I WANTED to know
how the mailman felt
on a cold, wintry day.
So I donned my coat
and went out into the cold stormy air.
The sharp snow smacked my cheeks
until they grew red.
My ears were cold and ached
as if pricked by needles;
My fingers were stiff and dead;
my toes seemed made of wood,

and the wind whistled through me
and chilled me to the bone.
I gasped for breath
as the gusts of wind swept past me.
I wanted to know
how the mailman felt.

I wanted to know
how the policeman felt
on this frosty day,
and I trod the sidewalks
until I could walk no longer.
Snow entered my shoes
and soaked my stockings.
The wet bothered me
and I longed to go back home,
back to the dry warmth,
but I kept on....
I wanted to know
how the policeman felt.

HERMAN ABROMSON. Aged 18.

BLOW, WIND, BLOW

BLOW, you wind,
Blow fiercely
And cut the skin of my face;
Blow hard

You devilish gust of air!
My heart is burning
With an unconquerable fire.
I am tired of the constant
Monotonous labor,
I am tired.
High is the peak of success
Far up in the clouds.
I am weary of reaching
For the rungs of the
Ladder of fame.
Blow, you wind, blow;
Lift me upon your wings and
Carry me on!

HERMAN ABROMSON. Aged 19.

HANDS

BY the hands of men I see their life.

There is the sculptor with fine fingers,
with hands that have power and strength,
hands that carve and send forth a spirit
of beauty in art,
Artist's hands.

There are my mother's hands,
rough yet delicate.

Rough from constant enduring work,
housework.
Hands that grope to give us
what she has not.
My mother's hands.

There is the laboring man's hand
that shows his crude work.
His thick dirty skin
cannot be pierced;
a skin that depicts life's progress,
life's toil.

All our hands show our life,
All our souls speak through our fingers.

HERMAN ABROMSON. Aged 18.

MY GRANDFATHER

MANY times thoughts of my grandfather
Come to me.
And upon shutting my eyes
I vividly see him.
A short rugged little man
With a graying beard upon his chin.
Upon his head a small cap
And from his shoulders
Hangs a long black cloak —

Sitting near a table
On Friday evening
Saying and singing
The 'Song of Songs'
As all pious Jews do on their Sabbath eve.

The candles lit for the day of rest
Stand before him
And cast his shadow upon the wall.
Large is the shadow
And it follows
The movements of my grandfather.

Time passes by
And the candles are flickering out.
As life ebbs away reluctantly
So do the candles
Flare up and down
Casting a gloomy shadow about the room.
My grandfather's head falls on his breast,
He is sleeping.
His loud snores frighten me
And I crawl into a corner,
Tuck myself against the wall
And also fall asleep.
The candles die out
And darkness fills the room.

HERMAN ABROMSON. Aged 19.

BOB

I KNOW Bob better than they —
I know him as he actually lives —
They know him as he exists.

Bob and I have long talks together,
No one is around,
All is quiet.
Bob pulls out his harmonica,
He plays.
Melancholy are the tunes
And I ask
What are you playing, Bob?
'Oh nothing;
I just feel funny.'
Melancholy are his songs
And the notes trill as he shakes
His hand against
The harmonica.

The melodies come from the soul of Bob;
From Bob
A creation of God
Not the drunkard, the bully of a gang,
The gambler, the flirter with girls.
Yes, I know Bob —
A soul-possessing fellow.

I hear him play the mouth-organ...
Songs,
Heart songs —
Bob's songs.

HERMAN ABROMSON. Aged 19.

BERUSH

EVERYONE in town knew Berush
the water carrier.
When anyone would see his stooped figure
ambling along under the burden of
a couple of pails of water,
he would point his finger and say,
'There goes Berush!'

He had a far-away gaze,
his pale face was covered
with a fuzzy beard
which he would scratch while
thinking over a problem.

The younger generation
called him a philosopher
and jovially would ask questions
and laugh at his crude answers.
Berush was by no means modest.
He would draw a circle of people

about him and pour forth
his 'philosophy.'
'When I have a short errand
I charge ten kopikos;
for a far errand I charge
five kopikos,
for on a short errand I cannot stop to rest
while on a far errand I rest on the way.
Such is life.'
And the listeners would nod their heads
urging him on.

As for me,
I will not question his philosophy,
but ah,
what a business man!

HERMAN ABROMSON. Aged 19.

WHEN YOU CAME

(TO ISADORE)

WHEN you came, my friend,
When you came back home
I was filled with excited joy.
My pulse beat fast, as my press ran on in the shop,
I turned on the full power and the machine kept
          pace with my mind.
All saw and cried

'Where is the fire, there,
Where is the fire?'
And I yelled out like a fruit peddler on the street
Shouting above the clanking of the press,
'In my heart, you devils,
In my heart!'

HERMAN ABROMSON. Aged 19.

CARUSO ON THE PHONOGRAPH

HER face
A slim white oval in the dusk
Was lifted.
Pitifully eager
The blind girl listened...
His voice was rich with tears.

DOROTHY AMDUR. Aged 14.

FOGHORN

SOMEHOW,
One of the things most sorely missed
On a night in the prairies
Is the voice of the foghorn
Stealing cool and forlorn
Across the mystic waters
From another world.

DOROTHY AMDUR. Aged 15.

SOMETIMES

I WATCH my shadow
Leap easily over a wall.
Sometimes I see it trail
Heavily behind me in the dust.

JACQUES AUSTRAL.

OF NIGHT

DARKNESS I treasure most:
It covers things I cannot understand
And leaves the things I love alone.

JACQUES AUSTRAL.

ALONE

I FEEL the shadow of my casement lengthen
— another night.
Long winding night-filled lanes
imbue the horror of desolation.
I wish the day were prolonged forever
darkness is too much the blind man's world.
Old thoughts swirl before my eyes
— all shrivelled up like wilted flowers.
I am alone again tonight.
Alone?
Now the long blue shadow of my casement pillar
is streaked with silver.

Tonight
> — alone again
> With the moon.

> JACQUES AUSTRAL. Aged 14 to 17.

MARCH NIGHTS

I CANNOT sleep nights, now that March is here;
The winds of heaven blow too wondrous free
Outside my door.
The driven rain makes too much harmony
Upon the grass and in my heart.
And I can think of naught, these sounding nights
> But quickening buds
> And dripping trees
> And wind-swept stars.

> HELEN BUCHMAN. Aged 17.

NOCTURNE

THEY say one catches many dreams
From broken points of stars at night,
Faint ones from stars we cannot see,
From larger ones, dreams rich and bright.

But let me have a bit of you,
Oh little star I scarcely see,
The thoughts that a child has in sleep
I wish that you would send to me.

The world may have its dreams of might
By plucking bits of ruddy Mars,
But I shall sleep the live-long night
With sweet, faint dreams from little stars.

HELEN BUCHMAN. Aged 17.

THEME AND VARIATIONS

I

MONOTONE is beautiful;
It fits within this span of time
With infinite harmony.
Unceasingly.

II

The monotone of rain is beautiful;
It leaves its cool wet footprints, even strides
Upon still consciousness.
Boundlessly.... .

III

The love I know is beautiful,
Sweet monotone of constancy,
High shining like a beacon,
Reaching even to eternity.
Infinitely....

HELEN BUCHMAN. Aged 17.

GROWN UP

My pockets were filled with such trivial things —
Glass marbles and skate-keys and tops without
    strings,
A penny or two, and once in a while
A comb with thin paper, my cares to beguile.

But my skirts have grown long, and my pockets
    grown small,
Till now there's a kerchief and comb, and that's all.
And now I've a longing for trivial things, —
Glass marbles and skate-keys, and tops without
    strings.

HELEN BUCHMAN. Aged 18.

EIGHTEEN

Eighteen, alone, and without light
Strides to the open gate;
Laughs — and scans the murky night;
Is gone and faces Fate.

And would that other mortals might
Have that youth's buoyant tread,
Nor shut out Life in timid fright
Nor make their way in dread.

JACK CHARLES. Aged 18.

FALSE SPRING

A WEEK ago I thought that spring was here,
And sang the dazzling turquoise of the sky;
But now the winter reasserts itself
And bitter words have given me the lie.

Cloudy days and fog and chilling winds
Have put an end to this, our early spring, —
But I could still have thought the winter gone
Had not your narrow words dulled everything.

JACK CHARLES. Aged 18.

MOONLIGHT

MOONLIGHT'S the same —
Whether it gleams through trees
Rustling in the faint mid-summer breeze,
Or if like flame,
White and yet heatless, glitters on the snow
With a weird glint of ages long ago
When there came
Those from the *Sidh* so stealthily to sing
The coming spring —
Moonlight's the same.

And the old moon
Wielding on me her goddess-given might

With steely light,
Winter or June,
Can make me blind to all I used to see
And steal my heart from me.

JACK CHARLES. Aged 18.

WHAT THIEF

THEY say a lover is the
Stealer of the heart
But tell me
What thief has stolen
My thoughts.

VERA CLARK. Aged 14.

IS IT FOR COLOR?

PLUMP pink peonies
Perching on capable toes,
Why do so many
Black ants come to visit?

VERA CLARK. Aged 14.

'THE DIAMOND SPARKLES ONLY IN THE LIGHT'

ALONE, companionless
You are fine in your
Singular beauty

Yet among relations
I find you ugly.

VERA CLARK. Aged 14.

PALS

FEAR is my companion,
He takes me everywhere.
He sits and wrinkles up my plaits
And ruffles up my hair.

He argues with me ever,
He always disagrees,
He gives me queer sensations,
Brings shakings to my knees.

I like him for his cowardice,
I love his disposition.
He comes to me quite dubiously
And asks for recognition.

Fear is my companion,
He takes me everywhere.
And you can always tell us
By our rude distrustful air.

VERA CLARK. Aged 14.

TREASURY

THE dripping rain is my silver,
The gleaming sun my gold.
The petaled flowers my jewels,
Such riches few behold.

I put them in a guarded mint,
They seem like gems to me,
Each placed within a thief-proof case
Known as my memory.

VERA CLARK. Aged 14.

FRUIT OF FAME

I STOOD and watched at your garden gate
And saw you eat your fruit of fame,
Fruit that you ate so ravishingly,
Fruit that was sweet to eat, I know.

I watched you eat so enviously,
I so hungry, stood without,
You said, 'Come in and taste my fruit,'
And I went nearly in.

Something there was that kept me out,
Kept me from entering your garden gate,
Told me to find the fruit of my own,

That only mine would be sweet to me.
I stand no more at your garden gate.
Not that I yet have found my own,
But somehow I know it will not be long
But that soon I too will be eating fruit.

ALICE M. CURTIS. Aged 17.

RIVERS

EVERY river has its beauty
When the sun's rays break upon it,
Even dirty Cuyahoga, with its lazy curves and
    ripples
Has its beauty,
Has a beauty all its own.

ALICE M. CURTIS. Aged 19.

FLITTING

I WILL go and leave you,
So quietly you will not know.
Sometime you will awake and call —
I shall not answer,
I shall be gone.

(Oh silver grass of the morning,
I am going far away.
Silver grass, sing me your song once more,

Of the wind playing in your leaves...
Before I am gone.)

ALICE M. CURTIS. Aged 19.

WINTER EVENING

SNOWFLAKES falling
Through the pallid sky;
Street lights gleaming,
And darkness... by and by.
As we walked together
Not so long ago
Through the glistening crunching
Solitary snow.
— As we talked together
In the misty night,
Snowflakes falling
Wrapped us in their white.
— Snowflakes falling
Only added to
The innocence untainted,
The beauty that was you.

MARY DEHEY. Aged 16.

TRAFFIC

MODERN fireflies
In the summer nights

Holler to each other —
'Put on your lights!'

MARY DEHEY. Aged 15.

THE CANDLE

So LIKE some struggling life it was
It sputtered out
With only a faint flicker at the end;
But I was not so much concerned with that
As with the dark —
The utter dark it left me in.

MARY DEHEY. Aged 15.

DOWNTOWN AT DUSK

LET'S go in and have an ice cream soda,
I'm starved, aren't you? — Oh, we'll be home on
        time;
And we can talk the whole show nicely over,
Wasn't it just... come along now, this treat's mine!
Let's go in and have a chocolate soda;
That little table at the side — you know,
And with the lamp above it in the corner,
Where we can watch the people come and go.
Let's go in please! Last time I was down here
I went in all alone without you there;
And folks just swarmed around me; — did I miss
        you?

I couldn't have been lonelier anywhere!
Oh — it's such a lovely time to loiter,
Now the downtown day is growing dim,
And little lights shine out from pretty windows,
Let's have a chocolate soda... let's go in!

MARY DEHEY. Aged 16.

ON PASSING A NEWSPAPER OFFICE

A BUSINESS man who hastily retreats
Behind enclosing, crisp newspaper sheets;
Workers who scan perhaps a page or more
Of unimportant print, and as before
So many times, are somehow satisfied.
Women soon laying the mussed folds aside,
And painted girls, to whom the paper brings
'Continued' shallow, syndicated things.
Life in a street-car, soggy, footsore, spent; —
This is that elusive element
'The Reading Public' — agents, salesmen, clerks,
— For these the paper works.

MARY DEHEY. Aged 16.

'IF NOBODY COMES TONIGHT...'

If nobody comes tonight,
(— And I hope nobody will)
By my little cozy light

I'll read, and maybe write,
— If nobody comes tonight,
And dream my idle fill.

If nobody comes tonight
(— And I hope nobody will)
My fire will burn as bright,
My room be not too still.
O rapturous delight!
Domestication quite...
If nobody comes tonight,
(But I know somebody will!)

MARY DEHEY. Aged 16.

EPITAPH FOR A COMMUTER

UNASKED, God's ticket agent, death, stood by,
And passed him, free, a one-way fare to die.

MARY DEHEY. Aged 17.

THE SUN IN POOLS

HAPPY showers
Leave silver pools
Upon sidewalks...
The morning sun
Falls into them
And I,

I dip my hands
Into the sun.

PHILLIP GARFIELD. Aged 19.

BIRCHES

I LIKE birches
When in the spring
They take to leaf...
I like their leaves; —
A green snow storm
That hesitates.

PHILLIP GARFIELD. Aged 19.

AWARENESS

I AM aware of memories
That darkness makes acute;
Hill birches fluttering down to meet the road,
Sunlight spinning veils of pale leaf-shadows.

I am aware that hopes I gathered
And kept secret, in the stillness,
Seem as frail as tree-etchings
Shivering on drowsy water;
That this intimate silence with myself
Is vastness of sky no mountain knows.
This is eternity that slips by

With ominous swiftness of deep rivers
And leaves me alone.

BERNICE GOETZ. Aged 18.

A CALL AFTER YOUTH

WHY am I calling after youth before
The years have told me that uncertain spring
Is gone? It seems a few young hours ago
That I could know a tall pine's breathless glimpse
Of sky, and walk through woods in seeping dusk
With light fawn steps.
                              But not this quietude
So soon, this tiredness that trees must know
In fall, of rivers during droughts, this slow
Erosion of rich earth. If youth must go,
Then give the sea my crystal dreams to pound
Against high cliffs and I shall listen for
Their broken music through the long slow years.

BERNICE GOETZ. Aged 19.

RECOLLECTION

TIME would drift away from me
Like thin fog in a wind
If it were not for
Three chicadees in the orchard
Dusting down blossoms of snow,

An echo of the sea I hear
Over winter-silenced hills,
And in my dreams, your voice
Calling ceaselessly.

BERNICE GOETZ. Aged 19.

A PAINTED LADY

THE years of her youth
Must have been blossoms too frail
For strong sunlight. Now
Their dried petals quiver in a breeze
With false ecstasy.

BERNICE GOETZ. Aged 19.

A PROSPECTOR OF HIGH PLACES

THE canyon walls shut out too much of sky
And tossed his mumblings harshly back to him.
So he was going back to his high places.
I watched him go, chiding his burro in
A voice high-pitched like winter winds that sweep
Through pines, peering with eyes that sun through
　　　　wraiths
Of snow had faded.
　　　　　　　Smoke of others' fires
Would rise to him like incense to a god.
And junipers would stretch their crooked arms

Toward him in age-long envy. There'd be nights
When rocks would seem slow-moving bands of elk
And starlight send swift shadows over drifts.
With lonesomeness to keep him company,
The mountains were sufficient for one life;
The blue rims in the distance were the end.

BERNICE GOETZ. Aged 19.

TWO WORLDS

ONCE I thought this world fair,
A fit sheath for me to
Slip the sword of my youth in.
But now
The world seems
An old gourd
In which little peoples
Like dried seeds
Rattle around uselessly.

LEAH GOLDMAN. Aged 16.

FOR ONE WHO DIED PEACEFULLY

HER life was full of calm beauty,
A large and perfect globe.
Each day a smaller globe
That spun peacefully within it.

LEAH GOLDMAN. Aged 16.

DESIRES

The wants of Man
Are as the growing greed
Of a miser
In a room filled to the brim
With gold.

Leah Goldman. Aged 17.

WHEN THE DAWN...

When the dawn poises herself
Over the sky
Like a virgin at the door of her lover's house:
The pure waters of morning
Come creeping over her feet,
Rose and orange and azure,
Covering their whiteness
With a translucent splendid tide.

Leah Goldman. Aged 17.

THE MOON

There's a silver sickle hanging
Near the frosted window pane,
That's always reaping clustered stars
And harvesting the rain.

Mary Louise Herbster. Aged 15.

TREASURE

MISTY dawns, and stars
And blue midnight
Are buried in my soul.

Splashing waves, and skies
And meadows in the sun
Are my dim goal.

Purple iris, against violet sky
And fresh dew
Are what I'm seeking for.

The flash of orioles in emerald boughs
May be a passing joy to you.
To me they're heaven's door.

MARY LOUISE HERBSTER. Aged 15.

BATTLE ROYAL

A VIBRATING whistle rent the night:
It was the stallion's battle cry.
On the hill in the pale moon light
His dancing form I could descry.
Strained and intense, I watched the fight
As two great kings in battle met:

The coiled serpent with poisonous bite
And the splendid stallion, black as jet.

Each struck at the other.   Each hit only air.
The struggle waxed hot as neither could gain.
But then I left, I did not care
To see the victor and the slain.
For I knew the victim conquered there
Would be the one I could not spare —
    The stallion.

AEOLA G. HUSTON. Aged 19.

LIFE RUMINATES

WHY do they hang to me —
These petty man-things?
Why must they close tenacious claws
Upon my snowy shining gown?
Strange, the way they clutch
When down beneath, in their Beyond,
A man can rest...
Why?

ROBERT JOYCE. Aged 16.

FAITH

IN the yard around her little shack
A 'Hunky' woman hangs her clothes to clean and
    dry.

(Behind her is the round-house where her husband
    works —
Beside her box-car home the coal piles lie.)

ROBERT JOYCE. Aged 16.

HOPE

A SHOOTING star swoops through the sky,
Red light against the dark in one sharp sudden
    swish.
A hobo sitting in the park is shown a flashing
    glimpse —
(He thinks of better times to come, and softly
    makes a wish.)

ROBERT JOYCE. Aged 16.

STANZA

DUST seeks dust in final rest,
Body and soul breast to breast,
United elements are pressed.
But prefaced with the life on earth
The spirit travels to rebirth.

LOIS JUDD. Aged 14.

NOW

FOG is a magician
Who curtains round my mind,

I cannot see before me,
Blackness is behind.
The Past has gone forever,
The Future's mystery,
For Fog's a shrewd magician
And the Present's all I see.

LOIS JUDD. Aged 14.

STREETS

CITY streets are queer things
That seem to run on without end.
Then like life, they stop abruptly
Where we read, 'Dead End.'

GERTRUDE KEDZERSKI. Aged 17.

TO RELUCTANT MORNING

MORNING, raise your arms,
Open your clenched hands,
Turn your palms — Dawn —
   To the world.

Morning, stretch your fingers
From their curved repose,
Thrust them — Sunrays —
   Upon the world.

Morning, lift your voice
From the depths of slumber,
Let it ring — Bird's Song —
   Around the world.

                DOROTHY KOSAK. Aged 17.

SHIPS IN THE MIST

THE fog horns on the lake tonight
Are whimpering dogs.
They circles walk, who have no sight
Like pool-whirled logs.

Unleashed, the swirling pack gives cry
To distant Mars,
Like them, abed I wonder why
We yearn for stars.

                SAMUEL KUTNICK. Aged 18.

LITTLE BOY BLUE

LITTLE BOY BLUE is fast asleep. He dreams
Perhaps, for would he smile, whose thin wan
    life
Has known the pettiness of lowly strife?
His tumbled locks are ringed — pale gold. Sun-
    beams
Filter through the blue hush of waning day

And linger on his battered cast-off horn.
In childish slumber he looks not forlorn
As when aware of worldly things. The hay
Sweet-smelling, soft as a mother's eyes, is home
To him who, ever homeless, had to roam.
So gently smiles he, lying on that heap
Of gold, that shy birds watch him in his sleep.

And still you cry, 'The sheep are in the corn,
Oh Little Boy Blue! Come... come blow your
      horn!'

SAMUEL KUTNICK. Aged 18.

RICHARD BLAINE

WE smiled when people spoke of Richard Blaine,
And sighed for what he was; — then smiled again
When our wives coughed and thought it looked like
      rain.
He knew no god nor creed nor social code,
In civic pride he had his lightest load,
Yet children laughed when passing his abode.
He worked to eat and did not eat to work.
He borrowed when he tired as a clerk,
But over winecups never did he shirk.
He mused on many distant idle things,
Like far-off lands and half-forgotten kings,
And why the child grown up, no longer sings.

Oh, we still smile (for years have passed in vain)
And sigh when people speak of Richard Blaine.

SAMUEL KUTNICK. Aged 19.
Reprinted from 'Bozart and Contemporary Verse.'

TROY

THE din of javelins rends the air,
Noise and shouts are everywhere,
Warriors by bold Odysseus led,
Fiercely attack and plunge ahead...
The boy reads and nods and dreams
Thinking of ancient Grecian schemes.

Thinking of long buried glories,
That are now retold in stories,
He sees the Iliad's cities fall,
A mass of ruins they are all;
The noisy rumbling of chariot wheels
The page before the boy reveals.
A thousand ships leave the Trojan bay,
They spread their sails and sail away.

JAMES LIOTTA. Aged 16.

THE LAST BUFFALO HERD

A MULTITUDE of shifting shadows
Moving ever in the gloom,

From a myriad shaggy hoofs
Comes a loud resounding boom.

With their mighty shoulders heaving,
Their drooping heads and sweep of horn,
They are plodding in the twilight
To vanish before the morn.

With their pounding, rushing feet;
Uncouth, primeval in their sway,
Surrendering to their destiny —
A creature that has had its day.

JAMES LIOTTA. Aged 16.

PIRATE

I WANT to be a pirate
On a black-hulled pirate ship;
With captured treasure in the hold
And Spanish oaths upon my lip.

I want to sail to a distant isle,
And hide my treasure there;
And make a map in pirate style
So that only I know where.

I want to sail the Spanish Main,
And seek untravelled ways;

I want to live just once again
The old romantic days.

JAMES LIOTTA. Aged 16.

DOLPHINS

DOLPHINS following the ship;
How they leap and flash and dip!
Mariners still the tale unfold
That they are ghosts of sailors old,
Sailors lost in the briny deep.
Awakening from their lengthy sleep,
Fishes receive the sailors' souls.
In a dolphin that leaps and rolls
Is the spirit of a sailor brave
Lost beneath the billowy wave.

JAMES LIOTTA. Aged 16.

PORTRAIT OF A STREET

ONLY the purring of the motors
And the slobbering of the wheels
Through the wet slush....
Only the thumping feet
Of the passing crowd
And the murmur of words
In many tongues.

JAMES LIOTTA. Aged 17.

WORDS

SHALL we forget the whispered word,
That you thought went by unheard,
The little mocking silent laugh
As vivid as a photograph,
The little upward tilt of chin,
The taunting word beneath the din?
A word you might have thought inane
Made another writhe in pain.
For words may oft be barbed things
A tongue in thoughtless anger flings,
And often too, words will return
And make the speaker's own heart burn
With the pangs of deep remorse —
You were the flinger! You the source
Of all the bitterness and tears.
Word ghosts linger through the years.

JAMES LIOTTA. Aged 17.

THEY TELL NO TALES

THEY tell no tales — who only know
The coolness of the earth below,
The silent blissfulness of sleep —
Of the tryst that they will keep
Somewhere far beyond the stars....
They tell no tales — and yet they must

Feel an urge within the dust,
A subtle urge that was a soul
A human soul that could not rest
Within a little earth compressed,
Souls of those who used to be
Longing for Eternity.

                          JAMES LIOTTA. Aged 18.

DUST SAYS

DUST says —
  I like old things —
    Old wines
    Old men
    Old names —
          Old alleys
          Old houses
          Old dreams.

                    LILLIAN V. MACKEN. Aged 19.

A SIGN

BEWARE of my explanations:
They are never made
To those I love!

                    LILLIAN V. MACKEN. Aged 19.

YOUR WORDS

Your words were bold
As love itself
          My Lady
They are
This water flame that leaps
To strike and spurn
And fall
          ... from rock!
Rock's members are humble
As love itself
          My Lady
He will wait
Until fury is become
          a mist.

Lillian V. Macken. Aged 19.

WALKERS AT DUSK

Here I lie with slippered feet,
Watching walkers on the street.
Footsteps, footsteps, childish, mannish,
Hurry past me, then they vanish.

Here I lie and mark each beat
To the even sound of feet.
No footstep enters my dark door
And lonely shadows come once more.

Hope B. Madison. Aged 17.

BEFORE SUNRISE

Why am I standing here
Before the wind-whipped glass
Watching the yellow dawn
Now softly, quickly pass?

The fishing boats draw seams
Across the shadowed bay,
Their motors quench the dawn —
Its peaceful quiet way.
The western skies still crouch
In unknown depths of sleep.
But soon, how soon, the sun
Out of the east will creep.

Hope B. Madison. Aged 17.

IN MEMORY OF M. V. B.

He hauled a sheet out of the chest
And said: 'There! Them's the sails
That was hoisted fifty years ago
To breast Atlantic gales.'
Once a sheet of creamy white
Stiff with salt sharp crust,
But now appearing to be
Lame and gray with dust.

Hope B. Madison. Aged 17.

SNOOZING

Chin lapped over turned-down sheet,
Face all washed and hair so neat,
Sapphire eyes now shut so tight,
Silent lips that said 'goodnight.'

Candle flame that's put to death
By his meager little breath.
Toward the doorway I now start
And leave him snoozing.   Bless his heart!

HOPE B. MADISON. Aged 17.

YOUR HEART'S DIARY

Your heart's diary
For long has been neglected.
You have made a few entries
But I know not what they are.
Oh, I beg of you
For one minute only,
Will you not open the cover
And show me the love within?

MARJORIE PATTISON. Aged 12.

ARCHÆOLOGY

A cave man trod over it;
The wind swept it with mud.

Aeons passed
Then I found it
And made a jewel
For you.

MARJORIE PATTISON. Aged 12.

LAKE ERIE

THE lake's face is that of an old, old man,
Covered with a million wrinkles.
But in body he is like a boy
Exulting in unsurpassed power
As he does what mischief he can.

MARJORIE PATTISON. Aged 13.

THE OUTCAST

You brace your strong shoulders
To the storm.
The winds part your mud-clotted mane.
People pass and remark
'Just another cur.'
But you aren't one to me.
I love your shagginess
And your clear bold eye.

MARJORIE PATTISON. Aged 13.

TIME LOST, ADMIRING

I ADMIRED him
Because I thought he was strong,
Never frightened,
Even by intangible things
Like darkness, eternity...
But then
He is so weak,
Afraid to look facts in the face,
Cringing,
Trying to hide
From his haunted mind.

MARJORIE PATTISON. Aged 14.

TO A DEER

HOLD the goodness of heaven
In your antlers.
Keep back the fires of hades
With your hoofs.
You are strong
And tall
And gracious.
Yet you can't do that.

MARJORIE PATTISON. Aged 13.

OUR CLOCK

I WONDER what our clock could tell
If it were only willing.
Perhaps it knows a lot of stories
Funny, sad, or thrilling.

I'd like to hear about its ride
Upon the mover's truck.
It must have taken courage
And a lot of grit and pluck.

I s'pose our clock would think it dull
To pore so over books.
When it sees me doing that
How stern and stiff it looks!

All night, while we are fast asleep,
The clock's our faithful guard.
It stays awake most all the time,
A task I think quite hard.

Occasionally it goes to sleep
And then we have to wind it.
I'd hate a waking up like that
But Clock just doesn't mind it.

Our clock is such a silent thing,
We don't know much about it.

The only thing it tells is time,
But could we do without it?

JOSEPHINE PEEBLES. Aged 17.

BRANCHES

BLACK fingers interlaced
Against the dim autumnal sky,
Fingers that are ever reaching upward
To grasp empty space:
Perhaps, tonight, they are merely pointing
To call my attention
To the somber beauty of the heavens,
That boundless depth of purple
Pierced here and there with silver.

LUCILLE STENDER. Aged 19.

MORNING

THE rising sun lifted an eyelid black
And grinned at the drowsy world.
From the yawning black chimneys
Of factory buildings
Long threads of smoke uncurled.
A queen's caravan
Shrouded in mist
Moved slowly across the sky.
And I caught a glimpse

Of her royal robes
Through the mists, as she passed by.

LUCILLE STENDER. Aged 16.

THE BALLOON MAN

ON the busy street corner
Where a flitting sunbeam
Gilds the battered tin cans
In the gutter,
The balloon man stands.

His tattered rags flap
About his gaunt scarecrow figure.
He stoops
As though his wares were heavy.

He gazes wistfully
At every passer-by,
And waves his bouquet
Of vari-colored bubbles enticingly,
But only little children care.

LUCILLE STENDER. Aged 16.

A NEW TIME

RELIEVED from winter toil
Freed from cumbersome coats

Swinging along at a merry gait
Laughing when meeting friends on your way,
Greeting the pattering rain
With a smile;
Happy because birds are happy,
Gay because springtime,
Love time
Is here.
Ah! Lift your eyes to the sky
And utter the song in your heart.

JULIA ELIZABETH VAN COURT. Aged 17.

TO D. T.

WANDERER, wanderer,
Where do you go?

I have seen
the high eager flying
of birds south... the blue
absorbing vanishing wings....

Wanderer, wanderer,
Do you go to warm lands?

I have seen
the flame flashes
of vivid sunsets sink
kisses into cool green water...

Wanderer,
Do you dream dreams that end in nothing?
Wanderer, wanderer,
What do you want?

    I have seen
       the proud moon grasped
          in fierce hands, only
             to slide through the fingers
               leaving trails of
                   white laughter....

Wanderer,
Do you want love you can never keep?

                        VIOLA L. WEIRICH. Aged 17.

LAMENT IN SPRING

EVEN Nature wars....

Summer trees are stripped in the
Fight against winter.

Standing exhausted in Spring,
Naked, bruised, passionate,
They lift sensitive, clinging hands
To a moody sun.

And the warm rain creeps down,
Caresses their slim sleekness,
Kisses their feet in glad reunion
... their faces... their praying hands.

Some songs return.
The trees whisper sadly,
'Ah, you cowards...'
But the same trees raise tingling hands
And fill them with those songs.

Even Nature wars...
But there comes peace...

Rain...
The snow yields...

Summer and Winter meet
With tears in Spring.

VIOLA L. WEIRICH. Aged 17.

LIST OF BOOKS

LIST OF BOOKS

Poetry in Theory and Practice:

Austin, Mary. *Everyman's Genius.* Bobbs Merrill.

Chapin, E., and Thomas, R. *A New Approach to Poetry.* University of Chicago Press.

Cox, Sidney. *The Teaching of English — Avowals and Ventures.* Harper and Brothers.

Eastman, Max. *The Enjoyment of Poetry.* Scribner.

Henri, Robert. *The Art Spirit.* Lippincott.

Lowes, J. L. *Convention and Revolt in Poetry.* Houghton Mifflin.

Munson, G. B. *Robert Frost: a Study in Sensibility and Good Sense.* Doran.

Richards, I. A. *Science and Poetry.* Norton.

Rylands, G. H. W. *Words and Poetry.* Payson and Clarke.

Sergeant, E. S. *Fire Under the Andes.* Chapter 14 on Robert Frost. Knopf.

Snyder, E. D. *Hypnotic Poetry.* University of Pennsylvania Press.

Stein, Leo. *The A.B.C. of Æsthetics.* Boni and Liveright.

Untermeyer, Louis. *The Forms of Poetry.* Harcourt Brace.

Poetry by Young People:

Conkling, Hilda. *Poems by a Little Girl*. Stokes.
     Shoes of the Wind. Stokes.
Mearns, Hughes. *Creative Youth*. Doubleday Page.
     Creative Power. Doubleday Page.

Poetry of Other Countries and Other Times:

Bynner, W. *The Jade Mountain*. Knopf.
Cohen, H. L. *Lyric Forms from France*. Harcourt Brace.
Colum, Padraic. *Anthology of Irish Verse*. Boni and Liveright.
Lowell, A., and Ayscough, F. *Fir Flower Tablets*. Houghton Mifflin.
Mackail, J. W., translator. *Select Epigrams from the Greek Anthology*. Longmans Green.
Masefield, John. *William Shakespeare*. Holt (Home University Library).
Van Doren, Mark. *Anthology of World Poetry*. Boni.
Waley, Arthur. *Japanese Poetry*. Clarendon Press, Oxford.

Poetry of the American Continent and its People:

Austin, Mary. *The American Rhythm*. Harcourt Brace.
Bynner, W. *Indian Earth*. Knopf.
Colcord, J. C. *Roll and Go*. Songs of American Sailormen. Bobbs Merrill.
Cronyn, G. W., editor. *The Path on the Rainbow*. Boni and Liveright.

Finger, C. J. *Frontier Ballads*. Doubleday Page.

Johnson, J. W. *God's Trombones*. Viking Press.

Lomax, J. A. *Cowboy Songs and Other Frontier Ballads*. Macmillan.

Rickaby, F. L. *Ballads and Songs of the Shanty Boy*. Harvard University Press.

Rourke, C. *American Humor*. Harcourt Brace.

Simpson, W. H. *Along Old Trails*. Houghton Mifflin.

Skinner, C. L. *Songs of the Coast Dweller*. Coward McCann.

Talley, T. W. *Negro Folk Rhymes*. Macmillan.

Walton, E. L. *Dawn Boy*. Dutton.